New Edition

Impact Issues 3

Richard R. Day

Joseph Shaules

Junko Yamanaka

Series Editor
Michael Rost

PEARSON
Longman

Published by
Pearson Longman Asia ELT

20/F Cornwall House
Taikoo Place
979 King's Road
Quarry Bay
Hong Kong

fax: +852 2856 9578
email: pearsonlongman.hk@pearson.com
www.pearsonlongman.com

and Associated Companies throughout the world.

This book was developed for Pearson Longman Asia ELT by Lateral Communications Limited.

First published 2009
Reprinted 2010 (twice)

Produced by Pearson Education Asia Limited, Hong Kong
SWTC/06

Project Director: Michael Rost
Project Editor: Allison Gray
Art Director: Keiko Kimura
Text Designer: Cindy Potter
Video Producer: Todd Rucynski
Production Coordinator: Richard Whitbread
Audio Engineer: Glenn Davidson
Website Coordinator: Keiko Kimura
Photographs: Bananastock, Blue Moon, Brand X Pictures, Dynamic Graphics, Getty Images, Iconotect, Inmagine.

Acknowledgements
The authors and editors of the series would like to thank the following people who provided reviews and piloting reports that aided us in developing
Impact Issues:

Benjamin Anderson
Steve Andrews
Jared Betts
Michelle Bird
Joshua Borden
Claude Carone
Robert Casanova
Marilyn Cawley
Li-ching Chen
Charles Chon
Jude Chung

Suzy Connor
Carol Ann Edington
Rebecca Elliott
Brett Elphick
Minyih Christine Feng
Glen Gainer
Timothy J. Gawne
Doreen Gaylord
Greg Goodmacher
Ken Hartmann
Mark Hawking

Louise Haynes
Tien-Hsin Hsin
Stella Hsu
Sylvia Hsu
Hideko Ino
Aaron Jolly
John Jurcin
Tomoko Kato
Linda Kilpatrick-Lee
Arram Kim
Tae Lee

Kelly McClusky
Niall O'Reilly
Wayne Allen Pfeister
Lesley Riley
Jason Rinaldi
Eric Ritholz
Cameron Romney
Christopher Ruddenklau
Stephen Ryan
Scott Scattergood
Helen Seo

Daniel Shin
Richard Snelson
Laurie Stuart
Daniel Thach
Joe Walther
Margaret Yamanaka
Candace Yu

We would also like to thank our colleagues at Pearson Education for their ongoing support, feedback, and guidance. We especially wish to thank Rachel Wilson, Richard Whitbread, Tom Sweeney, Eric Vogt, Katherine MacKay, SunMi Ma, Jan Totty, Serene Chiu, Borys Diakonow, Adrienne Glad, Michael Tom, and Steve King.

IMPACT ISSUES 1
Student Book with Self-Study CD ISBN 978-962-01-9930-1

IMPACT ISSUES 2
Student Book with Self-Study CD ISBN 978-962-01-9931-8

IMPACT ISSUES 3
Student Book with Self-Study CD ISBN 978-962-01-9932-5

Introduction

Impact Issues 3 is part of a 3-book series (*Impact Issues 1, Impact Issues 2, Impact Issues 3*) designed to help students develop conversation and discussion skills. *Impact Issues 3* is a complete course in oral communication for students at an intermediate level of English proficiency. It is a collection of 20 exciting and timely topics that students enjoy discussing. Each of the 20 units is carefully presented with activities designed to help students understand the topics, express their own points of view and opinions, and make short presentations.

Learning Philosophy

The *Impact Issues* series has developed a unique *content-based* and **student-centered** approach to language learning. The situation or story in each unit represents a *theme* that students reflect upon, discuss, and share their points of view about. The themes represent **personal issues**, such as life goals, ethics, friendships, romantic relationships, family ties, and jobs, as well as **social issues** such as equal rights, globalization, nationalism, environmental concerns, conflict and peace, refugees, and education.

The activities in *Impact Issues* are intended to help students develop in four key areas of language learning: **comprehension, critical thinking, self-expression,** and **motivation.**

Comprehension

Comprehension is the basis for all language development. The *Impact Issues* series helps students increase their comprehension ability through both **reading** and **listening**. Each unit is set up so that students can engage their **background knowledge**, work at identifying main ideas and supporting evidence, and **make inferences** about the speakers' points of view. Throughout the course, students are exposed to a wide range of speaking and self-expression styles and varieties of **international English**.

Critical Thinking

Critical thinking is the ability to **think deeply**, to go beyond explicit information. The *Impact Issues* series helps students develop and use the skills of **comparing information** from complementary sources and reflecting on **personal experience**. Each unit series focuses on both critical thinking skills and critical thinking attitudes.

Critical thinking skills enable students to weigh **different sides of an issue** and arrive at a fair judgment. Critical thinking attitudes allow students to show respect for others' opinions, appreciating **diverse values** and viewpoints and gain the **confidence** to think through an issue.

Self-Expression

Self-expression is the core of a communicative approach to language learning. The *Impact Issues* series focuses on both **discussion** and **presentation** skills.

The heart of each unit is the **sharing** of opinions with classmates, which includes conversation strategies such as soliciting ideas, getting **clarification** and **confirmation**, expressing levels of agreement, and adding evidence and examples to support students' own ideas.

Each unit concludes with a **short personal presentation**, to allow students to feel the power of self-expression in a new language. Students are guided in planning what to say, taking notes, outlining their ideas, and rehearsing.

Motivation

As students go through the process of understanding the issues, reflecting on the issues, discussing different points of view, and sharing their ideas, they will gain **communicative confidence**. Since the students are giving their personal point of view about the topics discussed, they gain a sense of **language ownership**—the sense that they can use English for meaningful communication. This makes the experience of studying English with *Impact Issues* motivating, so that students will want to **extend their communication** beyond the classroom.

Using *Impact Issues*

The units in *Impact Issues* are designed to be accessible linguistically, while challenging the students intellectually. *Impact Issues* is especially suitable for learners whose reading, grammar, and vocabulary skills are greater than their oral production skills. Each unit features a step-by-step preparation that turns students' passive knowledge into active communication practice.

Each unit has these sections:

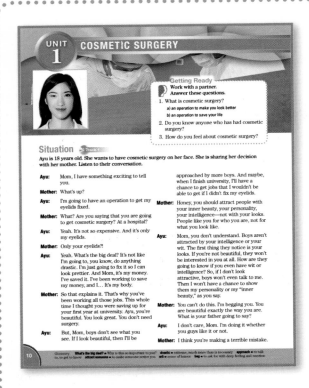

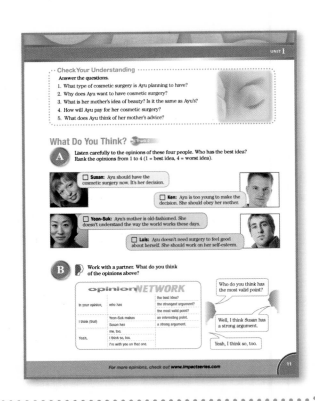

Getting Ready

Estimated time: **5 minutes**

- Introduces the topic and gets students thinking about their ideas and opinions about the topic.

- Students can work in pairs, taking turns asking and answering the questions. Alternatively, teachers can discuss the questions with the whole class.

Situation

Estimated time: **10-20 minutes**

- Presents the main issue of the unit.

- Students can read the story and listen to it on the Self-Study CD at the same time.

Check Your Understanding

Estimated time: **5 minutes**

- Checks students' understanding of key points.

- Students work in pairs to answer focus questions about the Situation.

What Do You Think?

Estimated time: **10 minutes**

- Helps students understand different perspectives and formulate their own opinions.

- Students work in pairs to share their opinions and expand ways of giving and responding to opinions (Opinion Network).

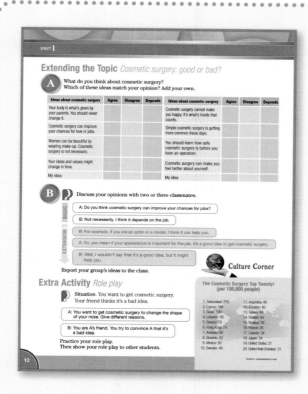

Extending the Topic

Estimated time: **10-15 minutes**

- Lets students connect the unit topic to broader issues and develop critical thinking.
- Students interact in a variety of communication formats: surveys, opinion exchanges, role plays, and debates.

Culture Corner

Estimated time: **5-10 minutes**

- Links the unit theme to a current topic.
- Students discuss cultural topics.

Sharing My Ideas

Estimated time: **20-30 minutes**

- Provides support for students in sharing ideas, in pairs or groups.
- Students work through 4 clear steps to prepare short presentations:

  1. **Choose:** select a topic of personal interest.

  2. **Prepare:** answer focus questions, complete charts and graphs, and write notes to make their ideas more specific.

  3. **Rehearse:** work in pairs to practice short presentations and give feedback to their partners.

  4. **Present:** present ideas again, to a new partner or to a larger group, while listeners complete a task.

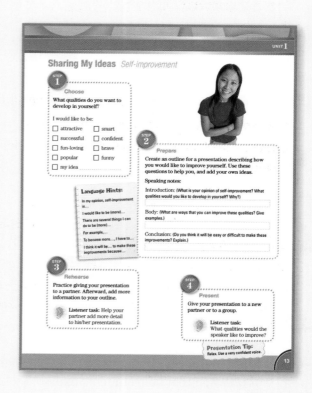

In the Appendix

Personal Opinions

- Provides unrehearsed opinions from a variety of speakers about each unit topic.
- Students complete a cloze exercise for the opinion summary. Full video clip available at www.impactseries.com/issues.

Vocabulary

- Provides additional vocabulary items and extended definitions of key words and phrases from the unit.
- Students study definitions from *Longman Dictionary of Contemporary English.*

Supplementary Resources

The *Impact Issues* support website (www.impactseries.com/issues) contains

- Unit-by-unit teaching tips

- Unit tests, semester tests, and final tests

- Commentary on units by the individual authors

- Inspirational monographs by the authors on the teaching of skills and development of successful learning attitudes and strategies

- Video clips of fluent English speakers giving extended opinions about each topic in *Impact Issues*

- Links to Internet sites that help teachers develop their own thinking about the topics in *Impact Issues* and that help students explore these topics further.

To the Student

Impact Issues will help you express your opinions and discuss topics in English *successfully*. You will also become confident in presenting your ideas and opinions. The topics and the situations are so interesting that you will want to say something. When you have something you really *want* to say, you learn to speak to the best of your ability.

Here are some tips to help you use *Impact Issues:*

Situation

- Imagine yourself in the situations and stories. How would you feel? What would you do? How can you solve the issue?
- Listen to the Self-Study CD. Think about each speaker's point of view.

What Do You Think?

- Listen to the opinions on the CD. Try to understand their ideas and feelings.
- Give your own opinion. Don't worry about making mistakes.
- Express your true feelings and talk about your own experiences. This is real communication.

Extending the Topic

- Study the example questions and responses. Memorize the patterns.
- Try new vocabulary and new phrases when you talk about your own opinions.
- Listen to new ways that people express their ideas.

Sharing My Ideas

- Speak up, even when you feel a little nervous! This is the fastest way to gain confidence.
- Challenge yourself! You will be able to make a lot of progress with your English when you try to say more.

Enjoy communicating in English.
By the time you finish Impact Issues, *you will be a powerful communicator!*

Contents

Unit	Synopsis	What Do You Think?	Extending the Topic	Sharing My Ideas
11. Naomi's Dilemma pages 50–53	A woman is uncomfortable because her boss asked her out to dinner.	Should employees go out with their bosses?	Business dinner or date?	Sexual harassment
12. No Place Like Home? pages 54–57	Two students abroad have very different reactions to their experiences.	How should we deal with culture shock?	Country pride questionnaire	Tour guide!
13. Career Choice pages 58–61	Two friends disagree on career choices and life goals.	Is money more important than lifestyle?	What's important when choosing a job?	Job interview—presenting yourself
14. Save Our Country pages 62–65	A "Shingistan" citizen warns about the "enemy" within his country.	Is Mr. Ware a racist?	Immigrant jobs	The rights of immigrants
15. High-tech Toys pages 66–69	A wife complains that her husband spends too much time with technology.	Does technology create distance in relationships?	High-tech lifestyle	Then and now
16. A Woman's Place pages 70–73	An expert discusses her belief that women belong at home.	Who should work and who should stay at home?	Societal roles	The ideal spouse
17. The Art of Compromise pages 74–77	A newlywed couple complains about each other's shortcomings.	How much should we compromise for a spouse?	Who is right?	Making a compromise
18. Can War Make Peace? pages 78–81	A teenager living in a war zone disagrees with his father about the war.	When is war justified?	War and peace—my philosophy	Conflict!
19. One-sided Love pages 82–85	A young man has fallen in love with his neighbor, but he's never met her.	Should we stop our friends from getting into trouble?	Is it love or stalking?	Make your own love story!
20. My Split Family pages 86–89	A high school student discusses the effect of his parents' divorce on him.	When is it OK to get a divorce?	Responding to Kenny	Decreasing the divorce rate

Appendix:
1. **Personal Opinions**—extra opinions about the topic of each unit. Corresponds to video clips available on the course website, www.impactseries.com/issues.
2. **Vocabulary**—expanded vocabulary items and definitions for each unit.

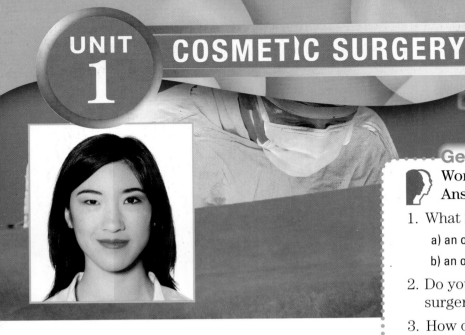

UNIT 1 COSMETIC SURGERY

Getting Ready

Work with a partner.
Answer these questions.

1. What is cosmetic surgery?
   a) an operation to make you look better
   b) an operation to save your life

2. Do you know anyone who has had cosmetic surgery?

3. How do you feel about cosmetic surgery?

Situation   ◁ Track 1

Ayu is 18 years old. She wants to have cosmetic surgery on her face. She is sharing her decision with her mother. Listen to their conversation.

Ayu: Mom, I have something exciting to tell you.

Mother: What's up?

Ayu: I'm going to have an operation to get my eyelids fixed.

Mother: What? Are you saying that you are going to get cosmetic surgery? At a hospital?

Ayu: Yeah. It's not so expensive. And it's only my eyelids.

Mother: Only your eyelids?!

Ayu: Yeah. What's the big deal? It's not like I'm going to, you know, do anything drastic. I'm just going to fix it so I can look prettier. And Mom, it's my money. I've saved it. I've been working to save my money, and I… It's my body.

Mother: So that explains it. That's why you've been working all those jobs. This whole time I thought you were saving up for your first year at university. Ayu, you're beautiful. You look great. You don't need surgery.

Ayu: But, Mom, boys don't see what you see. If I look beautiful, then I'll be approached by more boys. And maybe, when I finish university, I'll have a chance to get jobs that I wouldn't be able to get if I didn't fix my eyelids.

Mother: Honey, you should attract people with your inner beauty, your personality, your intelligence—not with your looks. People like you for who you are, not for what you look like.

Ayu: Mom, you don't understand. Boys aren't attracted by your intelligence or your wit. The first thing they notice is your looks. If you're not beautiful, they won't be interested in you at all. How are they going to know if you even have wit or intelligence? So, if I don't look attractive, boys won't even talk to me. Then I won't have a chance to show them my personality or my "inner beauty," as you say.

Mother: You can't do this. I'm begging you. You are beautiful exactly the way you are. What is your father going to say?

Ayu: I don't care, Mom. I'm doing it whether you guys like it or not.

Mother: I think you're making a terrible mistake.

Glossary **What's the big deal? =** Why is this so important to you? **drastic =** extreme, much more than is necessary **approach =** to talk to, to get to know **attract someone =** to make someone notice you **wit =** sense of humor **beg =** to ask for with deep feeling and emotion

Check Your Understanding

Answer the questions.

1. What type of cosmetic surgery is Ayu planning to have?
2. Why does Ayu want to have cosmetic surgery?
3. What is her mother's idea of beauty? Is it the same as Ayu's?
4. How will Ayu pay for her cosmetic surgery?
5. What does Ayu think of her mother's advice?

What Do You Think?

 A Listen carefully to the opinions of these four people. Who has the best idea? Rank the opinions from 1 to 4 (1 = best idea, 4 = worst idea).

☐ **Susan:** Ayu should have the cosmetic surgery now. It's her decision.

☐ **Ken:** Ayu is too young to make the decision. She should obey her mother.

☐ **Yeon-Suk:** Ayu's mother is old-fashioned. She doesn't understand the way the world works these days.

☐ **Luis:** Ayu doesn't need surgery to feel good about herself. She should work on her self-esteem.

  B Work with a partner. What do you think of the opinions above?

opinion NETWORK

		the best idea?
In your opinion,	who has	the strongest argument?
		the most valid point?
I think (that)	Yeon-Suk makes	an interesting point.
	Susan has	a strong argument.
Yeah,	me, too.	
	I think so, too.	
	I'm with you on that one.	

Who do you think has the most valid point?

Well, I think Susan has a strong argument.

Yeah, I think so, too.

Extending the Topic *Cosmetic surgery: good or bad?*

A What do you think about cosmetic surgery?
Which of these ideas match your opinion? Add your own.

Ideas about cosmetic surgery	Agree	Disagree	Depends	Ideas about cosmetic curgery	Agree	Disagree	Depends
Your body is what's given by your parents. You should never change it.				Cosmetic surgery cannot make you happy. It's what's inside that counts.			
Cosmetic surgery can improve your chances for love or jobs.				Simple cosmetic surgery is getting more common these days.			
Women can be beautiful by wearing make-up. Cosmetic surgery is not necessary.				You should learn how safe cosmetic surgery is before you have an operation.			
Your ideas and values might change in time.				Cosmetic surgery can make you feel better about yourself.			
My idea:				My idea:			

B Discuss your opinions with two or three classmates.

BASIC

> A: Do you think cosmetic surgery can improve your chances for jobs?

> B: Not necessarily. I think it depends on the job.

EXTENSION

> B: For example, if you are an actor or a model, I think it can help you.

> A: So, you mean if your appearance is important for the job, it's a good idea to get cosmetic surgery.

> B: Well, I wouldn't say that it's a good idea, but it might help you.

Report your group's ideas to the class.

Extra Activity *Role play*

Situation. You want to get cosmetic surgery.
Your friend thinks it's a bad idea.

> A: You want to get cosmetic surgery to change the shape of your nose. Give different reasons.

> B: You are A's friend. You try to convince A that it's a bad idea.

Practice your role play.
Then show your role play to other students.

Culture Corner

The Cosmetic Surgery Top Twenty!
(per 100,000 people)

1. Switzerland: 215
2. Cyprus: 186
3. Spain: 100
4. Lebanon: 85
5. Greece: 78
6. Hong Kong: 74
7. Australia: 66
8. Slovenia: 52
9. Mexico: 50
10. Sweden: 48
11. Argentina: 45
12. Ecuador: 45
13. Taiwan: 44
14. Finland: 44
15. Norway: 35
16. France: 35
17. Canada: 34
18. Japan: 34
19. United States: 31
20. United Arab Emirates: 31

Source: nationmaster.com

Sharing My Ideas *Self-improvement*

STEP 1

Choose

What qualities do you want to develop in yourself?

I would like to be:

- ☐ attractive
- ☐ smart
- ☐ successful
- ☐ confident
- ☐ fun-loving
- ☐ brave
- ☐ popular
- ☐ funny
- ☐ my idea ....

STEP 2

Prepare

Create an outline for a presentation describing how you would like to improve yourself. Use these questions to help you, and add your own ideas.

Speaking notes:

Introduction: (What is your opinion of self-improvement? What qualities would you like to develop in yourself? Why?)

Body: (What are ways that you can improve these qualities? Give examples.)

Conclusion: (Do you think it will be easy or difficult to make these improvements? Explain.)

Language Hints:

In my opinion, self-improvement is…

I would like to be (more)…

There are several things I can do to be (more)…

For example,…

To become more…, I have to…

I think it will be… to make these improvements because…

STEP 3

Rehearse

Practice giving your presentation to a partner. Afterward, add more information to your outline.

 Listener task: Help your partner add more detail to his/her presentation.

STEP 4

Present

Give your presentation to a new partner or to a group.

 Listener task: What qualities would the speaker like to improve?

Presentation Tip:
Relax. Use a very confident voice.

Getting Ready

Work with a partner.
Answer these questions.

1. Who is your best friend?
2. How did you meet your friend?
3. What do you do together?

Situation Track 3

Keiko and Akira have been friends for a long time. But they might not be friends any longer. What has happened to hurt, and maybe even end, their friendship? Listen to their story.

Akira and I were leaving the university library after several hours of studying for an exam, something we often do together. We stopped to say good night.

"Good night, Akira. See you tomorrow. I know you'll do well on the test."

Akira took me by surprise. "Keiko, let me kiss you good night. Come here, come close to me."

"What are you doing, Akira?" I asked, hardly able to speak. "You are my best friend. We have been friends for five years. You are closer to me than my brother. And now you want to kiss me?"

"Yes, very much. I want our friendship to be even closer," Akira said.

"No, no, no! I don't think of you in that way. You are my friend. Best friends don't act that way," I said.

Then Akira said, "What, Keiko? I'm confused... I don't understand. Don't you see me as a man?"

"Of course you are a man. And a handsome man, Akira. But you are a special man—my best friend.

But we can't do this. Don't you understand?" I tried to explain myself to him, but he still didn't understand.

He said, "No, not at all, Keiko. Here is how I see it. You are a woman and I am a man. We like each other very much. We are very close to one another. So let's do what is natural in any male–female relationship."

I said, "Natural? I think our friendship is natural. I thought I understood you, Akira. Maybe I was wrong."

"So you really don't like me at all! You just want someone to talk to. Well, Keiko, find someone else to talk to. I'll find a woman who sees me as a man."

Akira turned and walked away quickly. As I walked to my apartment, I thought about what had happened and I felt so sad. In my heart, I knew that Akira was wrong. Men and women can be friends without being lovers. But maybe I was wrong. What if all men think like Akira? I don't know.

⋯ **Check Your Understanding** ⋯⋯⋯⋯⋯⋯⋯⋯

Are the sentences true or false? Circle T, F, or NI (not enough information).

1. Keiko and Akira have been friends for four years.   T / F / NI
2. Akira wants to marry Keiko.   T / F / NI
3. Keiko sees Akira as her brother.   T / F / NI
4. Akira will look for a girlfriend and stop seeing Keiko.   T / F / NI
5. In her heart, Keiko believes that men and women can be friends without being lovers.   T / F / NI

What Do You Think? Track 4

A   Listen carefully to the opinions of these four people.
Check all of the opinions you agree with.

☐ **Iris:** Keiko should tell Akira how she feels. Maybe he feels the same way.

☐ **Shingo:** Keiko and Akira should try being a couple. A strong friendship is important in any romantic relationship.

☐ **Mark:** Keiko should find her own boyfriend.

☐ **Anna:** Keiko and Akira should spend some time away from each other.

B   Work with a partner.
Discuss the opinions above.

opinion NETWORK

I	agree with Mark.	Keiko needs to find her own boyfriend.
	think Mark is right.	
Yeah,	I think	that's a good idea.
		you're right.
Really?	I don't think	that's such a good idea.
		so.

> I agree with Mark. Keiko needs to find her own boyfriend.

> I think that's a good idea. It looks like her friendship with Akira is over.

Extending the Topic *Can they be best friends?*

A What are some common opinions about why men and women can or cannot be best friends? Why? Complete the chart.

Reasons why they can be best friends	Reasons why they cannot be best friends
We are all humans.	They are very different.
Men and women can complement each other.	Women want someone to talk to intimately.

B Share your reasons with two or three classmates.

BASIC

> A: I think men and women can be best friends. What do you think?

> B: I'm not sure. I think it's really hard for a man to be best friends with a woman.

EXTENSION

> A: What makes you say that?

> B: Well, women and men are very different. I don't think they really understand each other.

> A: But what about marriage? Men and women can get along as a married couple. Why not as best friends?

Report your group's results to the class.
Does your group agree? Why or why not?

Extra Activity *Role play*

 Situation: Keiko is asking her friend for advice. She's confused about Akira.

> Keiko: 1. Explain exactly what happened with Akira.
> 2. Ask for advice using questions such as:
> • "Should I end my friendship with Akira?"
> • "Will his feelings change?"
> • "What should I do?"

> Keiko's friend: Listen to Keiko's story.
> Give her some advice.

Perform your role play in front of other students.
Compare the advice.

 Culture Corner

Attitudes about Male and Female Friendship

1. Do you believe men and women can be "just" friends?
   Yes: 83% No: 11% Unsure: 6%

2. Have you had a friendship that crossed the line and became romantic or sexual?
   Yes: 62% No: 36% Unsure: 2%

3. Is it possible to fall in love with someone who first enters your life as a friend?
   Yes: 94% No: 4% Unsure: 2%

4. Do you hope that when you do fall in love, your partner will have started out as your friend?
   Yes: 71% No: 9% Unsure: 20%

5. Who is better at keeping sex out of a friendly relationship?
   Men: 13% Women: 67% Unsure: 20%

Source: *Psychology Today*

Sharing My Ideas *My best friend*

STEP 1

Choose

Select one topic:

☐ Who is your best friend now?

☐ Who was your best friend when you were a child?

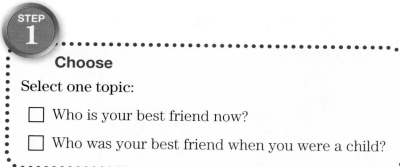

Language Hints:

Use adjectives to describe your best friend:

funny, interesting, helpful, understanding, honest, creative, energetic, outgoing, shy…

STEP 2

Prepare

Make notes about your best friend. Use the questions to help you.
Speaking notes:

1. What is/was your best friend's name? ....
2. Is/Was your best friend a male or a female? ....
3. How did you meet? ....
4. How long have you been/were you friends? ....
5. What is/was your best friend like? ....
6. Why is/was this person your best friend? ....

STEP 3

Rehearse

First, practice saying your ideas silently. Improve your notes. Then practice with a classmate.

 Listener task:
What adjectives did your classmate use in describing his or her best friend?

STEP 4

Present

Present your ideas to a new partner or to a group.

 Listener task: What reasons does the speaker give for having that person as a best friend?

Presentation Tip:
Speak clearly. Don't speak too fast or too slowly.

Getting Ready

Work with a partner.
Answer these questions.

1. What is global warming?
2. What are some causes of global warming?

Situation Track 5

Dan and Bob share an apartment. They disagree about the use of the air conditioner in their apartment. Listen to their conversation.

Dan: Bob, did you change the air conditioning again?

Bob: Yes.

Dan: Why did you change it? The temperature in the apartment was perfect, just as I like it.

Bob: I know how you like the temperature: cold, colder, and coldest! I changed it because you changed it.

Dan: Yes, that's right. I did change it. I hate how you like the temperature: hot, hotter, and hottest! I can't stand a hot apartment!

Bob: The temperature was 18 degrees! Dan, that's cold. Think of the energy that the air conditioner uses to keep the apartment at 18 degrees.

Dan: Who cares? I just want to be comfortable.

Bob: Comfortable? You're wearing a sweater now. When the AC is set at 25 degrees, you don't have to wear a sweater. And you help stop global warming.

Dan: What do you mean? How does setting the AC at 25 help stop global warming?

Bob: OK, when we keep the AC at a low temperature, the AC uses a lot of energy, and that will produce a lot of CO2. CO2 is one of the major causes of global warming. So if we make the temperature of the AC a few degrees higher, we will save energy and help to save the Earth. Think about the future of our planet, Dan.

Dan: Well, I don't care about global warming. I don't care about saving energy. I like to be comfortable, Bob. One person cannot stop global warming. So I will do what I want. And I want to be comfortable.

Bob: So you want to keep the apartment cold? You don't care about saving energy or about global warming?

Dan: You've got to chill out, Bob. Don't worry about global warming. Scientists will find a solution. Now, please change the AC to 18.

Bob: If we set the AC back to 18, I WILL be chilled, Dan.

Dan: Great. Let's do it, then.

Bob: You just don't get it, do you?

Glossary   **air conditioning** = machine that controls the temperature indoors   **CO2** = carbon dioxide, a gas   **chill out** = to relax; to take life easy

·· **Check Your Understanding** ·······························

Answer the questions.

1. What season is it?

2. Who likes a cold apartment? A hot apartment?

3. What is Dan wearing? Why does this upset Bob?

4. How does having a higher temperature setting on the AC help stop global warming?

5. What is Dan's answer to global warming?

What Do You Think? Track 6

Listen carefully to the opinions of these four people. Who do you agree with most? Rate their ideas from 1 to 4 (1 = strongly agree, 4 = strongly disagree).

☐ **Ken:** Scientists will find a solution to global warming. We don't need to worry about it.

☐ **Luis:** The Earth is warming quickly. We need to be careful because it's our personal responsibility.

☐ **Susan:** One person can make a difference in helping to stop global warming.

☐ **Yeon-Suk:** I'm not even sure global warming is real. Some scientists say it's not really happening.

Work with a classmate.
Talk about the opinions above.

opinionNETWORK

	agree most		Luis.
	completely agree		him.
I	sort of agree	with	Ken.
	kind of agree		him.
	strongly disagree		Susan.
	don't agree at all		

I agree most with Ken. We don't have to worry about global warming.

I strongly disagree with him. I think Luis is right.

Extending the Topic *What can we do?*

A What can each of us do in our daily lives to help stop global warming?
Fill in the table. Add your own ideas.

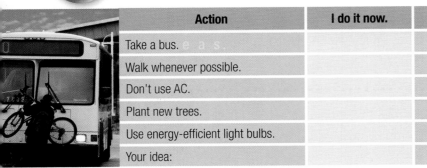

Action	I do it now.	I will do it.	I might do it.	I'll never do it.
Take a bus.				
Walk whenever possible.				
Don't use AC.				
Plant new trees.				
Use energy-efficient light bulbs.				
Your idea:				

B Talk about your ideas with two or three classmates.

BASIC

A: Well, I already take the bus every day. I guess I could buy some energy-efficient light bulbs. What are you going to do?

B: I'm not sure. I know I'll never plant any trees.

EXTENSION

A: Why can't you plant a tree?

B: I live in the city. I don't have a yard. Where am I going to plant a tree?

A: Most cities have a tree-planting organization. You should look it up online.

What were your group's best idea's for stopping global warming?

 Culture Corner

Extra Activity *Debate*

 Work in a group of 5.

Pair A: You believe that we need to try our best to stop global warming.

Pair B: You believe that we don't have to worry about global warming.

The Judge: Listen to their reasons.

First, Pair A and Pair B work with your partners.
Make a list of your reasons.

The Judge: Which pair made the better argument?

CO2 Emissions Around the World

World total CO2 emissions in thousands of metric tons: 27,245,758 ☞100%

• United States	6,049,435	22.2 %
• China	5,010,170	18.4 %
• European Union	3,115,125	11.4%
• Russia	1,524,993	5.6 %
• India	1,342,962	4.9 %
• Japan	1,257,963	4.6 %
• Germany	808,767	3.0 %
• Canada	639,403	2.3 %
• United Kingdom	587,261	2.2 %

Source: wikipedia.org

Sharing My Ideas *Disagreements*

Dan and Bob can't agree on the air-conditioner setting in their apartment. When people share a living space, they often disagree on how things should be. Think about a problem you had with a roommate or with a family member.

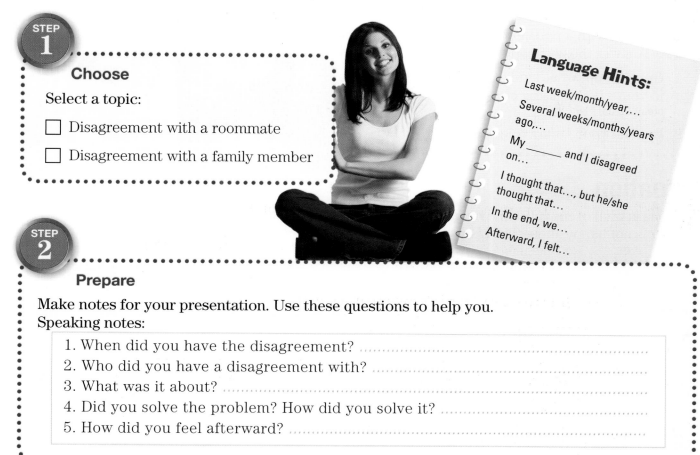

STEP 1

Choose

Select a topic:

☐ Disagreement with a roommate

☐ Disagreement with a family member

Language Hints:

Last week/month/year,...

Several weeks/months/years ago,...

My ____ and I disagreed on...

I thought that..., but he/she thought that...

In the end, we...

Afterward, I felt...

STEP 2

Prepare

Make notes for your presentation. Use these questions to help you.
Speaking notes:

1. When did you have the disagreement? ....
2. Who did you have a disagreement with? ....
3. What was it about? ....
4. Did you solve the problem? How did you solve it? ....
5. How did you feel afterward? ....

STEP 3

Rehearse

Work with a classmate. Practice your presentation.

 Listener task:
Do you understand what the disagreement was?
Do you want to know more about it?

Presentation Tip:
Use your notes, but look at your audience. Don't read word for word.

STEP 4

Present

Present your ideas to a new classmate or to a group.

 Listener task: Write the answer to these questions:

1. What was the problem? ....
....
2. Was there a solution? What was it?
....

RULES, RULES, RULES

•••• **Getting Ready** ••••••••••••

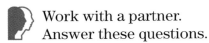

Work with a partner.
Answer these questions.

1. Growing up, what kind of rules are/were there in your family? (dating, phone calls, curfew, meals, cleaning up)

2. Explain your family rules.

Situation Track 7

Ramona is tired of the rules that her parents set for her. On this day, she is coming home late. Her mother is not happy about this. Listen to their conversation.

Mom: Ramona, where have you been? It's 11:30!

Ramona: I was just out with some friends.

Mom: But you know the rules, you are to be in by 10:00 unless you call.

Ramona: C'mon, Mom, nobody comes home that early. Do this! Don't do that! I'm fed up with your rules.

Mom: We've talked about this already. Your grades have been terrible. You spend your time at your part-time job and with your friends, so you never study. That's simply not acceptable.

Ramona: But I need to work because you don't give me enough money. What am I supposed to do?

Mom: You spend too much money shopping and going out. And your cell phone bill is really expensive. If you were more responsible, you wouldn't need rules.

Ramona: I just want to do things with my friends like everyone else.

Mom: And by the way, do I smell cigarettes on your breath? Have you been smoking? You know we've agreed that you aren't going to smoke.

Ramona: We agreed? No, you made another rule. Anyway, so what if I was smoking? Everybody does it.

Mom: Listen. It's for your own good. You'll thank me and your father someday. If you can't be responsible for a few simple rules here at home, how do you expect to do well in life?

Ramona: Do well in life? You always push me to do what you want. Be the perfect daughter, study hard, succeed, make you proud. No, I have my own life! What if I don't want to live like you and Dad?

Mom: You CAN live your own life. But you need to learn to follow a few rules first.

Ramona: You're impossible!

Mom: Listen to me. We know it's hard for you to understand. But we just want what's best for you.

Ramona: No, I do understand. You just want to control everything I do.

Glossary   **fed up with** = really tired of   **acceptable** = good enough; satisfactory   **push someone** = to put pressure on someone to do something

•• **Check Your Understanding** ••

Complete the sentences. Circle a, b, or c.

1. Why was Ramona's mother upset when Ramona arrived home?
   a) Because Ramona came home late.   b) Because Ramona didn't say she was going out.
   c) Because Ramona was supposed to study that day.

2. Why must Ramona come home by 10:00?
   a) Because it's dangerous late at night.   b) Because her grades have been bad.
   c) Because her mother doesn't like Ramona's friends.

3. How does Ramona feel about smoking?
   a) She's never tried it.   b) She thinks it's bad.   c) She thinks it's OK.

4. What does Ramona's mother think Ramona needs in order to succeed in life?
   a) To stop staying out late.   b) To be nicer to her mother.
   c) To learn to follow rules.

5. How does Ramona feel about the rules at home?
   a) She knows they're good for her.   b) She wants to follow them but forgets sometimes.
   c) She thinks they stop her from living her own life.

What Do You Think? Track 8

A

Listen carefully to the opinions of these four people.
Check all of the opinions that you agree with.

☐ **Mark:** Ramona's parents are just trying to teach her to be responsible.

☐ **Anna:** Ramona and her mother need to learn to communicate better.

☐ **Shingo:** Those rules seem a bit strict, but that doesn't mean Ramona should ignore them.

☐ **Iris:** Ramona's parents need to give her some freedom. They are trying to control everything.

B

Share your opinions with a classmate.
Discuss the opinions above.

opinion**NETWORK**

Shingo	thinks	the parents' rules are too strict.
	says	
Do	you	think he's right?
		agree with him?
Yes,	I	think he's right.
		agree with him.
No,		think he's wrong.
		disagree with him.

Shingo thinks the parents' rules are too strict. Do you agree with him?

Yeah. I think he's right. They are going too far.

Extending the Topic *A serious problem?*

 A Imagine you are the parent of a teenage child. Do you consider these problems serious? Add your own ideas.

☹ very serious   😐 somewhat serious   ☺ not serious

If my teenage child...	I think this problem is...			If my teenage child...	I think this problem is...		
talks on the phone a lot	⊗	😐	☺	starts drinking	⊗	😐	☺
often comes home very late	⊗	😐	☺	starts smoking	⊗	😐	☺
gets bad grades	☹	😐	☺	doesn't help with household work	☹	⊗	☺
has friends I don't like	☹	⊗	☺	plays video games a lot	⊗	😐	☺
my idea:	☹	😐	☺	my idea:	☹	😐	☺

 B Discuss your opinions with two or three classmates. Which of these problems is serious? What can you do to solve the problem?

BASIC

> A: Do you think it's a problem if your teenage child talks on the phone a lot?

> B: No, I don't think that's a very serious problem.

EXTENSION

> A: Why is that?

> B: Well, young people like to talk to their friends. It's normal.

> A: What would you do?

Report your group's ideas to the class.
What were your solutions to the problems?

Extra Activity *Debate*

 Work in a group of 5.

> Pair A: You believe that teenage children should follow family rules."

> Pair B: You believe that parents should give their teenage children some freedom."

> The Judge: Listen to their reasons.

Pair A and Pair B make a list of your reasons.
Then, exchange ideas with the other pair.

> The Judge: Which pair made the better argument?

 Culture Corner

 **Good Mother and Daughter Relationships**

Advice for daughters
1. Involve your mom in your life.
2. See your mom as she is to others.
3. Remember that she will always be your mommy.

Advice for mothers
1. Stop criticizing.
2. Give your daughter some space.
3. Remember the relationship you had with your mother.

Source: lifescript.com

Sharing My Ideas *Introducing... me as a child!*

STEP 1

Choose

Select your title:

☐ How I was as a child

☐ How I have changed

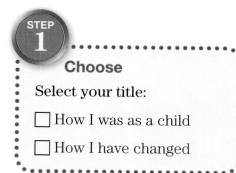

Language Hints:

When I was a child, I...

I really liked...

One of my favorite memories is...

I have changed a lot in many ways...

For example, I was..., but now I am...

STEP 2

Prepare

Make an outline.

Speaking notes:

Introduction (Say what you are going to talk about.)

Check the specific items that you will talk about:

☐ things I did

☐ things I liked

☐ who I lived with

☐ my room

☐ a special memory

☐ my childhood dream

☐ then and now

Conclusion (Make a final point about your childhood or how you've changed.)

STEP 3

Rehearse

Silent preparation: Close your eyes. Visualize memories from your childhood.

Speaking practice: Practice your presentation with a classmate.

 Listener task: After listening, ask questions about your partner's childhood.

STEP 4

Present

Present to a different classmate or to a group. Add extra details to your story.

 Listener task: Ask a follow-up question about something your partner said.

Presentation Tip:
Show your emotion. Use gestures and facial expressions.

Getting Ready

Work with a partner.
Answer these questions.

Plagiarism is when you pretend that someone else's words or ideas are your own.

1. Have your teachers ever explained plagiarism to you?

2. What do you think is the appropriate punishment for plagiarism at your school or university?

Situation ◁ Track 9

Peter's roommate Kan needs help with his writing. Peter suspects that he has plagiarized. Listen to their conversation.

Peter: Kan, I looked at the paper you wrote for your class.

Kan: Thanks for checking the English. Did I make a lot of grammar mistakes?

Peter: Your grammar is pretty good, but did you write everything in this paper?

Kan: Of course I did. Why?

Peter: You only have a couple of references in the paper, but the ideas you introduce look like they were taken from a book or something.

Kan: Well, um... I guess I did get some ideas from this one book. But that's research, right?

Peter: If you copy word for word, you have to use quotations. But even if you simply take ideas from somewhere, you have to show clearly whose ideas they are. You can't give the impression that YOU came up with them.

Kan: Well, it was just a kind of inspiration.

Peter: Really? In some places there are whole paragraphs that look directly copied from somewhere. The sentences are perfect and very difficult. It's hard to believe you wrote it.

Kan: Umm... Well, I can take that out. No big deal.

Peter: Look, you're plagiarizing. The university is very strict about that. If they catch you, you'll fail the class. You could even get kicked out of school.

Kan: Well, I was just trying to get good ideas. Maybe you can help me fix it. You know, improve it?

Peter: Sorry, but I can't help you. School rules say that students have to report anyone they suspect to be plagiarizing.

Kan: Look, I'm sorry. You know studying in English is hard for me. You know I study a lot.

Peter: That's true. But I can't help you with your papers anymore. I could get in trouble.

Kan: But I have to hand this in this afternoon!

Peter: I'm sorry, Kan. You'll have to find someone else.

Kan: You don't understand. I cannot fail this course!

Peter: Sorry. I just can't help you.

Glossary **reference** = source of information **give the impression** = to make people believe **plagiarize** = to pretend that someone else's words or ideas are your own **strict** = making sure rules are followed or obeyed **be kicked out** = to be forced to leave

·· Check Your Understanding ·····

Answer the questions. Circle a, b, or c.

1. Why did Peter look at Kan's paper?

   a) Kan had asked him to.   b) Peter just happened to see it.   c) They are in the same class.

2. Why does Peter think Kan is plagiarizing?

   a) Kan told him that he did.   b) Kan asked him how to do it.   c) Some things in the paper didn't seem right.

3. How does Peter feel about plagiarizing?

   a) He thinks it's OK.   b) He's against it.   c) He also does it sometimes.

4. What does Peter decide to do about Kan's paper?

   a) He will help him fix it.   b) He won't help him anymore.   c) He's not sure what to do.

5. Why did Kan say he plagiarized?

   a) He made a mistake.   b) He thinks it's OK.   c) English is hard for him.

What Do You Think? Track 10

 A

Listen carefully to the opinions of these four people.
Check all of the opinions you agree with.

☐ **Luis:** Kan should do his own work. Peter's right not to help him anymore.

☐ **Ken:** Peter is cruel. Kan just doesn't understand how to write papers correctly.

☐ **Yeon-Suk:** Kan should be more careful, but Peter shouldn't stop helping him.

☐ **Susan:** What Kan is doing is understandable. It's hard to study in a foreign language.

 B

Work with a classmate. What do you think of the opinions above?

opinion NETWORK

Luis	thinks	Peter's right not to help Kan anymore.
	believes	
I	think so, too.	
	have the same opinion.	
	believe the same thing.	
	don't think so.	
	don't think that's true.	
	disagree.	

> Luis thinks Peter's right not to help Kan anymore.

> Yeah. I have the same opinion. Kan should do his own work.

Extending the Topic *Helping a friend*

A What would you do to help a friend? Read the situation and decide what you would do.

You are in a car that your friend is driving. Your friend is driving too fast and hits another car. The person in the other car suffers some minor injuries. No one saw the accident. The police ask you how fast your friend was driving. If you tell the truth, your friend will get in serious trouble. If you lie, your friend won't be punished. What would you do?

☐ I would tell the police the truth and not protect my friend.

Reason: ....

....

☐ I would lie to the police to protect my friend.

Reason: ....

....

B Work with two or three classmates. Tell them what you would do.

BASIC

A: What would you do?

B: I guess I would tell the police the truth.

EXTENSION

A: Why?

B: Because it's not fair to the person who was hurt.

A: What do you think your friend would want you to do?

Report your group's ideas to the class.
Who had the best reasons for telling the truth?
For protecting the friend?

Extra Activity *Role play*

Situation: A police officer asks you about the accident.

A: You are a police officer.
B: You are the person in your friend's car.

Police officer, ask B questions about the accident.
For example:
• How fast was he/she going?
• Is he/she usually a careful driver?

Practice your role play. Then show your role play to other students.

Culture Corner

Avoid plagiarism — Checklist!

1. You must acknowledge someone else's material.

2. Quoting: Is the quotation exact?

3. Paraphrasing and summarizing:
   • Have you used your own words and sentence structure?
   • Do you use quotation marks when you use the author's exact language?

4. Is each use of someone else's material acknowledged in your text?

5. Does your list of works cited include all sources you have drawn from?

Adapted from *The Little Brown Handbook*, 7th ed., New York: Longman, 1998, p. 579

Sharing My Ideas *Nice guys finish last!*

Does being nice help you succeed in life? Talk about your philosophy on success.

STEP 1

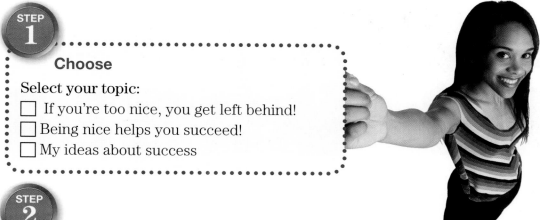

Choose

Select your topic:
- ☐ If you're too nice, you get left behind!
- ☐ Being nice helps you succeed!
- ☐ My ideas about success

STEP 2

Prepare

Organize your presentation by making an outline. Use these questions to get started.
Speaking notes:

> What is success for you?
> Do you like competition?
> What kind of people succeed?
> What is the key to success for you?

Introduction:

Body:

Conclusion:

Language Hints:

First, I'll talk about…

Next,…

Another thing is…

My main point is…

In conclusion,…

STEP 3

Rehearse

Practice with a partner.

Listener task: What connecting expressions did you hear?

STEP 4

Present

Give your presentation to a new partner or to a group. Use gestures to emphasize your important points.

 Listener task: What gestures did you see the speaker use?

Presentation Tip:
Using gestures and body language will make your presentation more interesting.

Getting Ready

Work with a partner.
Answer these questions.

1. When you were a child, who did most of the housework?

2. Which housework tasks do you like to do? Which do you hate?

Situation ◉ Track 11

Hye-Jin has a problem with her boyfriend, Kwan. She writes a letter to a famous doctor, Dr. Moon, asking for her advice. Listen to their conversation.

Dear Dr. Moon,

My boyfriend and I have a problem, a big problem. First, let me tell you that we're in love and want to get married. Our families agree to the marriage, too. Now, here's the big problem: housework! This is the one thing that we can't agree on. Both of us work and we plan to continue working after getting married. Kwan is old-fashioned and says he'll not do any housework after we get married. He says that housework is women's work. He says his father never does housework and that his mother does it all. He won't listen to me when I say that times have changed a lot since his parents got married. Most of my married friends say that their husbands share the household duties. And I don't want to be like his mother!

I have been trying to persuade him to help me with the housework, but he refuses. It's really not fair. He just doesn't understand how important this is to me. Should I marry him or not marry him? Marry him and just do all the housework? Marry him and hope he changes his mind? Or simply not marry him UNTIL he changes his mind?

What should I do?

Hye-Jin

Dear Hye-Jin,

I agree with you that it would not be fair. Kwan's mother does all of the housework, but she does not have a job outside the home.

You're right. Times have changed. Now many married women have responsible jobs. Their husbands should not expect them to do all of the housework.

Think about these possibilities.

First, calculate all of the time you would spend cleaning and all of the expenses housework would cost in one month. Show Kwan that. Make him realize that housework is not free. But if he still doesn't want to help you, then both of you should pay to hire housework professionals.

Finally, if Kwan refuses to pay his share, then tell him that he must do the housework!

Of course, this third possibility might postpone the wedding.

Good luck!

Dr. Moon

·· Check Your Understanding ··········

Answer the questions.

1. What is Kwan's reason for not doing housework?
2. Why does Hye-Jin want Kwan to help with the housework?
3. What does Hye-Jin say about her married friends?
4. What does Dr. Moon say about Kwan's mother?
5. What is Dr. Moon's advice to Hye-Jin?

What Do You Think? Track 12

 A

Listen carefully to the opinions of these four people.
Check all of the opinions you agree with.

☐ **Shingo:** Husband or wife, whoever is better at housework should be mainly responsible.

☐ **Mark:** When both wife and husband work outside the house, they can hire professionals to do the housework. That's the best way.

☐ **Iris:** Housework is women's work. Sorry, that's just the way it is. Not going to change.

☐ **Anna:** They should each do half of the housework. Isn't that fair?

 B

Work with a partner.
Talk about your ideas.

opinion NETWORK

How do you feel about	Mark's	opinion?
		argument?
		point?
I	understand	what she means.
	know	how she feels.
	don't	understand her point of view.
		know what she's talking about.

How do you feel about Mark's opinion?

I know how he feels. Hiring a professional is definitely the best solution.

Extending the Topic *Whose job is it?*

 A In your experience, who usually does these household tasks? Is it fair?

Task	Man	Woman	Both	Is it fair?	Task	Man	Woman	Both	Is it fair?
washing dishes				Yes / No	taking care of the baby				Yes / No
doing laundry				Yes / No	earning money for the family				Yes / No
cooking				Yes / No	cleaning the house				Yes / No
taking out the garbage				Yes / No	managing finances				Yes / No
going grocery shopping				Yes / No	changing light bulbs				Yes / No
My idea:				Yes / No	My idea:				Yes / No

 B Share your experiences with two or three classmates.

BASIC

> A: Who usually washes the dishes?

> B: In my house it depends.

EXTENSION

> B: If I cook dinner, my husband washes the dishes. If he cooks dinner, I do.

> A: That sounds fair.

> B: Yeah. It works for us!

Report your group's ideas to the class.
What were some "fair" situations that you talked about?

Extra Activity *Debate*

Work in pairs.

> A: You believe that life is easier for women.
> *Tip: Think of ways in which it's easier to be a woman.*

> B: You believe that life is easier for men.
> *Tip: Think of ways in which it's easier to be a man.*

Prepare your debating points.
Make notes about what you want to say.

A and B debate in front of another pair.
When they are finished, the other students judge
the winner.

 **Culture Corner**

Housework Done by Men and Women

	Men	Women
• Australia	39.1%	70.3%
• Czech Republic	32.2%	28.6%
• France	30.9%	78.3%
• Israel	29.7%	75.1%
• Mexico	36.2%	70.4%
• Russia	35.8%	68.6%
• Sweden	36.3%	67.3%
• United States	37.3%	70.6%

Source: *Journal of Family Issues*; self-reported data

Sharing My Ideas *A letter to Dr. Moon*

STEP 1

Choose

Think of a problem you have (or someone you know has).

Examples:

- A friend is always late.
- Your roommate takes things without asking.
- Your boyfriend/girlfriend doesn't spend enough time with you.

What is your problem?

....

STEP 2

Prepare

Look at Hye-Jin's letter to Dr. Moon. Try to write a letter like hers.

Speaking notes:

Introduce the person with the problem:

....
....

Present the problem:

....
....

Explain how you've tried to solve the problem:

....
....

Describe the person's reaction to your idea:

....
....

Ask Dr. Moon for her advice:

....
....

Language Hints:

I have a big problem. I...

I have tried to...

...doesn't understand/won't listen to me.

Should I...?

What should I do?

STEP 3

Rehearse

Exchange your letter with a classmate. See if it has the parts above:

1. Person with the problem.
2. The problem.
3. Your classmate's solution.
4. Other person's reaction.
5. Question(s) for Dr. Moon.

STEP 4

Present

Read your revised letter to another classmate.

 Listener task: You are Dr. Moon. Give your classmate some advice.

Presentation Tip:
Take a deep breath. Try to relax.

Getting Ready

Work with a partner. Answer these questions.

1. Is abortion legal in your country? What are the laws concerning abortion?

2. Are you comfortable talking about this topic? Why or why not?

Situation Track 13

Mali has learned that she is pregnant, but she isn't ready to have a baby. What should she do? Listen to her problem.

My name is Mali. I'm only 19 years old, but I'm facing an impossible decision. I've been dating my boyfriend Lee for three months. A few days ago I learned that I'm six weeks pregnant. I was so shocked and I don't know what to do.

I love children and hope to have a family. But I don't know Lee that well and I'm not sure if I really want to marry him. I haven't told him that I'm pregnant because I'm not sure how he would react. He might deny any responsibility. Would he offer to marry me? I'm not sure.

My parents would be horrified if they learned that I am pregnant. They might even tell me to leave the house. They are rather traditional and probably wouldn't understand. If that happened and Lee didn't want to marry me, I would be at a total loss. I have no idea where I could go or what I could do. Another problem is school. I would have to quit university to take care of the baby. Since Lee is also a student, he might have to quit school, too.

My best friend Lena thinks that I should get an abortion. She says that the baby will not be happy with such a difficult family life. She says I made a mistake but that I shouldn't ruin my life by bringing a baby into an unhappy situation. If I get an abortion, I can continue my life as though nothing had happened. It would be my little secret.

My head tells me that this might be the best solution, but my heart is torn. In my heart, I believe that abortion is wrong and normally I'm against it. I can't imagine taking the life away from a baby before it's born. Could I forgive myself? Will I regret it if I don't? Should I ask Lee about it? Should I tell my parents? The only thing I know for sure is that I can't wait long before deciding.

Glossary   **pregnant** = carrying an unborn baby inside the body   **shocked** = very surprised   **deny responsibility** = to refuse the duty (of being a father)
horrified = shocked in a very negative way   **to have an abortion** = to end a pregnancy   **my heart is torn** = emotionally, I can't decide

••• Check Your Understanding •••••••••••••••••••••••••••••

Answer the questions. Circle a, b, or c.

1. Who knows about Mali's pregnancy?
   a) just her family   b) just her boyfriend   c) no one

2. How does Mali feel about her boyfriend?
   a) She loves him a lot.   b) She wants to marry him.   c) She's not sure if she loves him.

3. How does Mali feel about being pregnant?
   a) confused and worried   b) angry   c) surprised but happy

4. Why is Mali worried about her family's reaction?
   a) They are traditional.   b) They told her not to have a boyfriend.   c) She doesn't get along with them.

5. What is Mali going to do about her pregnancy?
   a) get an abortion   b) keep the baby   c) She doesn't know.

What Do You Think? Track 14

 A Listen carefully to the opinions of these four people. Who has the best idea? Rank the opinions from 1 to 4 (1 = best idea, 4 = worst idea).

 ☐ **Yeon-Suk:** Mali should tell the truth to her parents and to Lee.

 ☐ **Susan:** I'm afraid that Mali will regret having an abortion if she does.

 ☐ **Ken:** It's sad, but an abortion is the best option in Mali's case.

 ☐ **Luis:** Mali and Lee should get married and bring up the baby together.

  B Work with a classmate. What do you think of the opinions above?

opinion NETWORK

Ken	has	a good argument.
		a strong point.
Yeah,	I think	so too.
		he's right.
Really?	I	don't think so.
		disagree with him.

I think Ken has a strong point. What do you think?

Yeah. I think he's right. She's so young and she doesn't really know Lee.

Extending the Topic *Ending a pregnancy: right or wrong?*

A Mark whether you agree with these statements about abortion.
1 = strong agreement, 2 = agreement, 3 = disagreement, 4 = strong disagreement.

Abortions should...	1	2	3	4	Abortions should...	1	2	3	4
never be allowed.	☐	☐	☐	☐	be allowed but not too easy to get.	☐	☐	☐	☐
be free and easy to get.	☐	☐	☐	☐	only be allowed to save the life of a mother.	☐	☐	☐	☐
only be allowed in extreme cases like rape.	☐	☐	☐	☐	be every woman's right.	☐	☐	☐	☐
my idea:	☐	☐	☐	☐	my idea:	☐	☐	☐	☐

B Discuss this issue with two or three classmates. Give reasons for your answers.

BASIC

A: Do you agree with the idea that abortions should never be allowed?

B: Yes, I strongly agree. I don't think anyone should have an abortion.

EXTENSION

A: Why do you feel that way?

B: Because every human life is precious. Every baby deserves a chance in life.

A: You have a point, but what about the mother?

Report your group's ideas to the class. What is your group's overall opinion on abortion?

Extra Activity *Debate*

Work in groups of 4.

Background: In over 50 countries in the world, abortion is illegal or extremely limited.

Debate question: Should we fight to make those countries change their laws and allow abortion?

Pair A: Yes, we should.

Pair B: No, we shouldn't.

In pairs, prepare your debating points. Exchange your ideas with the other pair. Discuss whose arguments are stronger.

Culture Corner

Ending Pregnancies: Restrictions Around the World

Red: Extremely restricted   Pink: Very restricted
Yellow: Restricted   Blue: Relatively unrestricted
White: Easily available

Source: womenonwaves.org

Sharing My Ideas *My future family*

What kind of family life do you want to have in the future?

STEP 1

Choose

Select one topic:

☐ How many children I want

☐ My future family life

Language Hints:

Explaining:

I think children are... because...

There are several reasons why I believe this.

First,... Second,... Third,...

The reason why I feel this way is...

STEP 2

Prepare

Make notes. Use the questions to help you. Give your reasons.

Speaking notes:

How do you feel about children? ....

Reason: ....

How many children do you want? ....

Reason: ....

What is the best age to start a family? ....

Reason: ....

What is the secret to having a happy family? ....

Reason: ....

My ideas: ....

Presentation Tip:
Be enthusiastic! Try to put feeling into your voice.

STEP 3

Rehearse

Practice with a partner. Don't look at your notes while you are speaking.

 Listener task: After listening, use the feedback phrase, "Please explain more about... "

STEP 4

Present

Give your presentation to a new classmate or to a group.

 Listener task: After listening, use the feedback phrase, "I agree with what you said about... "

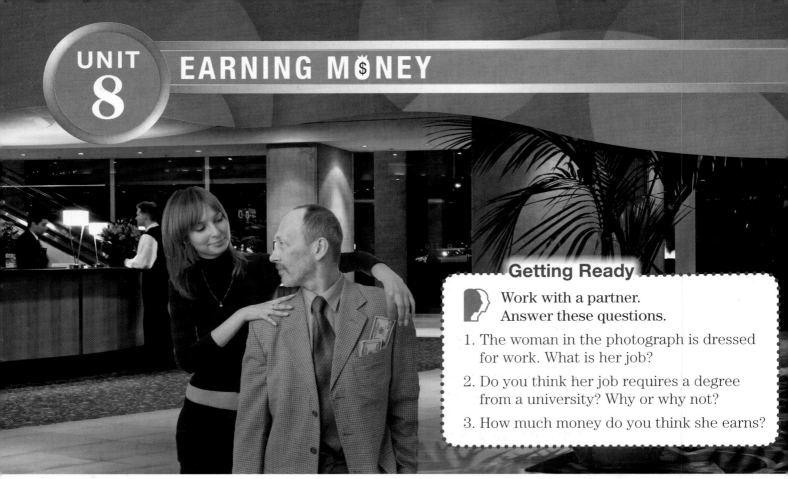

Getting Ready

Work with a partner.
Answer these questions.

1. The woman in the photograph is dressed for work. What is her job?

2. Do you think her job requires a degree from a university? Why or why not?

3. How much money do you think she earns?

Situation Track 15

May is a 24-year-old woman with two jobs. Does she like her jobs? Listen to her story.

I hate my day job—I'm a waitress. It's boring. The same thing, day after day after day. Taking orders from customers, smiling, being polite even when I don't like the people.

I really don't like my night job, either—I'm an "escort." But it's not boring, like my day job, and the pay is great! Men pay me to be their dates. They take me to dinners, concerts, bars—everywhere. I work hard, four nights a week. And I work on the weekends.

I started my night job without really thinking about being an escort. One day at lunch-hour rush, one of the customers in the restaurant asked me for a date. I don't know why, but I accepted his invitation. That night, he took me to an expensive restaurant. And after dinner, we went to a concert. And later, he gave me a lot of money to pay for my time. He wasn't handsome—he was actually quite a bit older than me, and not in very good shape.

Why am I an escort? To earn money. That's all. And I earn a lot of money every year. I use the money to buy nice clothes and to travel. And last year, I bought my parents a new house. They think I am only a waitress, so they were pretty surprised.

Do I like being an escort? Well, it's just my night job. There are always men who want to pay to be with beautiful women. So I have all the dates I want. And, well, I'll confess, it's kind of fun to realize the power that a young attractive woman has over most men.

Someday, I will get married and have children—just like other women. And my job as an escort will be something of the past. I won't tell my future husband. But until that day comes, I am going to continue with my day job and my night job.

Glossary   **escort** = a person who is paid to go on a date   **lunch-hour rush** = very busy time during the middle of the day   **confess** = to admit

Check Your Understanding

Are the sentences true or false? Circle T, F, or NI (not enough information).

1. May works as a waitress during the day.   T / F / NI
2. May earns a lot of money at her day job.   T / F / NI
3. May started her night job to earn money.   T / F / NI
4. May is going to look for a new job soon.   T / F / NI
5. May is married and has children.   T / F / NI

What Do You Think? Track 16

A Listen carefully to the opinions of these four people.
Check the opinions that you agree with.

☐ **Iris:** It's wrong for women to have dates with men for money.

☐ **Mark:** A woman can do anything she wants.

☐ **Anna:** It's OK for men or women to be escorts.

☐ **Shingo:** A man should find a real date, not an escort.

I agree with Iris. Women should not date for money.

B Share your opinions with a classmate.

opinion NETWORK

I	agree that	a man should find a real date, not an escort.
		women should not date for money.
Yes,	I think that's true.	But it's not always easy to find a date.
	I agree with that too.	But escorts can make a lot of money.

Yeah. I think that's true. But it's not a always easy to find a date.

Extending the Topic *What would you do for money?*

A May is an escort to earn money. Would you do these things for money?

Job / Activity	Yes, of course.	I'd consider it.	No way!	Job / Activity	Yes, of course.	I'd consider it.	No way!
escort				subject for medical research			
drug dealer							
nude model				race car driver			
soldier				erotic dancer			
my idea:				my idea:			

B Work with two or three classmates. Tell them what you would do.

BASIC

> A: Would you consider being an escort if you needed the money?

> B: Yeah. Sure, why not?

EXTENSION

> B: I really don't think it's a big deal. Would you consider it?

> A: No way! I would never date for money. People who hire escorts are desperate.

> B: That's not always true.

Report your group's ideas to the class. Who is the most daring? Least daring?

Extra Activity *Debate*

 Work in pairs.

Point of view: It's wrong for a woman to go on a date with a man just for money.

> A: I agree.

> B: I disagree.

Make notes of ideas to support your position.

Exchange your opinions. At the end of your debate, ask your partner, "Whose arguments do you think were stronger?"

 **Culture Corner**

Ten Most Popular Careers in the US, the UK, and Canada

- Network Systems Analyst
- Physician's Assistant
- Medical Assistant
- Medical Records and Health Information Technician
- Software Engineer
- Physical Therapist Aide
- Fitness Trainer
- Database Administrator
- Veterinary Technician
- Dental Hygienist

Source: alec.co.uk

Sharing My Ideas *Men and women at work*

Choose

Select one of the topics:

☐ Women and men (have/don't have) the same job opportunities.

☐ Women and men (can/can't) do the same jobs.

Language Hints:

I believe/I think that...

I feel this way because...

For example,...

In conclusion/To sum up,...

Prepare

Make notes. Give examples to support your position.

Speaking notes:

Introduction: (State your position)

Body: ....

Reason: ....

Example 1 ....

Example 2 ....

Example 3 ....

Conclusion: (Summarize your ideas) ....

....

Ideas to help: pay, education, type of work, balance with home life

Rehearse

Find a classmate who has the same position as you. Give your presentation.

 Listener task: What examples does your classmate give to support his or her position?

Present

Give your presentation to a classmate who has a different position.

 Listener task: What reason(s) does the speaker give for his or her position?

Presentation Tip:
Don't forget to smile!

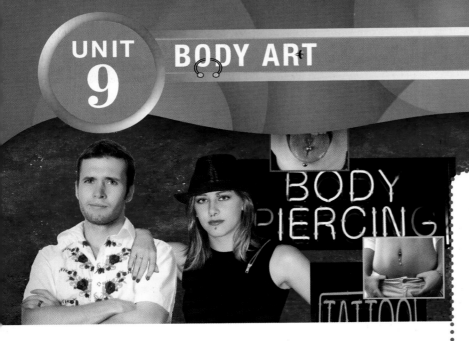

Situation Track 17

David had a fight with his girlfriend, Liz. He thinks her body art is unnatural, but David's friend Kevin doesn't agree. Listen to their conversation.

Kevin: Hey, David, you look down. Is everything OK?

David: Not really. I had a fight with Liz.

Kevin: Wow, what about?

David: It seems kind of silly, but it's about piercings. You know, her piercings.

Kevin: What do you mean?

David: I told her that they don't look good.

Kevin: Why'd you tell her that? She looks great, really hot! You're lucky to be with her.

David: Yeah, I know she's pretty, fun to be with, energetic... but those piercings! She had her nose pierced when I met her, but then she pierced her eyebrows and her belly button. And then she got her tongue pierced.

Kevin: Yeah, I noticed. It must be cool when you kiss her.

David: No, it isn't! It feels weird. Piercing your body isn't natural. And don't you think she looks kind of cheap?

Kevin: No way! Everybody has piercings these days. What did she say?

David: She got really mad. She told me to stop telling her what to do with her body. Then she said to me she was thinking about getting a tattoo.

Kevin: Cool! Where?

David: What do you mean, "cool"? You agree with her?

Kevin: You're totally overreacting. It's body art. She's making her body beautiful.

David: But it's NOT beautiful. Besides, everybody will look at her.

Kevin: Lighten up. You know what I think? You should try it, too! Get a piercing!

David: Oh, not you, too! That's what Liz told me! She said I would look really good with pierced ears.

Kevin: If it turns her on, why not do it?

David: Are you serious?

Kevin: You can't let something so minor get between you and the woman of your dreams.

David: I can't believe you're on her side! What am I going to do?

Kevin: You're going to get a piercing!

Glossary   **you look down** = you look sad   **hot** = very attractive   **weird** = strange   **overreacting** = responding too strongly
loosen up = to relax   **turns (her) on** = she thinks it is attractive   **minor** = unimportant

•• **Check Your Understanding** ••••••••••••••••••••••••••••••

Answer these questions. Circle a, b, or c.

1. Why did David have a fight with Liz?

   a) He didn't want to get a piercing.   b) He said her piercings don't look good.   c) He told her he didn't like tattoos.

2. What does Kevin think about Liz?

   a) That she is very attractive.   b) That she is a bit wild.   c) That she is not good enough for David.

3. How does Kevin feel about Liz getting a tattoo?

   a) He thinks she's going too far.   b) He thinks it's art.   c) He thinks it will look cheap.

4. What did Liz tell David?

   a) That he should get a piercing.   b) That he should get a tattoo.   c) That he doesn't understand her.

5. What does Kevin tell David to do?

   a) Find a new girlfriend.   b) Get a tattoo.   c) Get a piercing.

What Do You Think? Track 18

 A   Listen carefully to the opinions of these four people. Check the opinions you agree with.

☐ **Luis:** What's David's problem? He's got a great girlfriend! He should stop complaining.

☐ **Yeon-Suk:** David is behind the times. If he's not careful, Liz will break up with him.

☐ **Susan:** I agree with David. People with piercings and tattoos do look cheap.

☐ **Ken:** Liz sounds kind of pushy. She should care more what her boyfriend thinks.

  B   Work with a partner.
Discuss your opinions.

opinion*NETWORK*

What do you think of	Luis's	opinion?
How do you feel about		point?
I guess	he's right.	
	he has a point.	
I don't know.		
I'm not sure.		

What do you think of Luis's point?

I guess he's right. Liz seems like a great girlfriend. What do you think?

Extending the Topic *Looking beautiful*

A People have many different ways to make themselves beautiful. Do you think piercings and tattoos are a natural way to make your body look good? Give your opinion.

What do you think about...	It looks nice.	It depends.	It doesn't look good.	What do you think about...	It looks nice.	It depends.	It doesn't look good.
girls with pierced ears?	☐	☐	☐	guys with pierced ears?	☐	☐	☐
girls who wear makeup?	☐	☐	☐	guys who wear makeup?	☐	☐	☐
girls who have a tattoo?	☐	☐	☐	guys who have a tattoo?	☐	☐	☐
girls who color their hair?	☐	☐	☐	guys who color their hair?	☐	☐	☐
my idea:	☐	☐	☐	my idea:	☐	☐	☐

B Discuss your opinions with two or three classmates.

BASIC

A: What do you think about girls with pierced ears?

B: I think it looks nice. Lots of girls have pierced ears. What do you think?

EXTENSION

A: I agree. I think pierced ears are attractive, but other piercings are disgusting.

B: Why don't you like body piercings?

A: It just looks unattractive. Some people take fashion too far.

Share your group's ideas with the class. Which things does your group agree on?

Extra Activity *Role play*

Situation: Liz tries to convince David to get a tattoo with her.

Person A: You are Liz.

Person B: You are David.

Liz, ask David questions about getting a tattoo.
For example:
• What's wrong with getting a tattoo?
• Do you think it will hurt?

Practice your role play.
Then perform your role play for another pair.

Culture Corner

Top Ten Tattoo Designs

Tribal		Cherry Blossom	
Dove		Kanji	龍
Butterfly		Star	
Cross		Rose	
Lotus Flower/ Water Lily		Angel	

Source: vanishingtattoo.com

Sharing My Ideas *Fashion king! Fashion queen!*

STEP 1

Choose

Select a presentation title:

☐ My Fashion Philosophy   ☐ Fashion? Who cares!

STEP 2

Prepare

Make an outline about fashion and looking good.

Speaking notes:

Introduction: (Say what you are going to talk about.)

Body: (Give at least 3 reasons and examples.)

1. Reason: ....

   Example: ....

2. Reason: ....

   Example: ....

3. Reason: ....

   Example: ....

Conclusion: (Make a final point about your topic.)

....

....

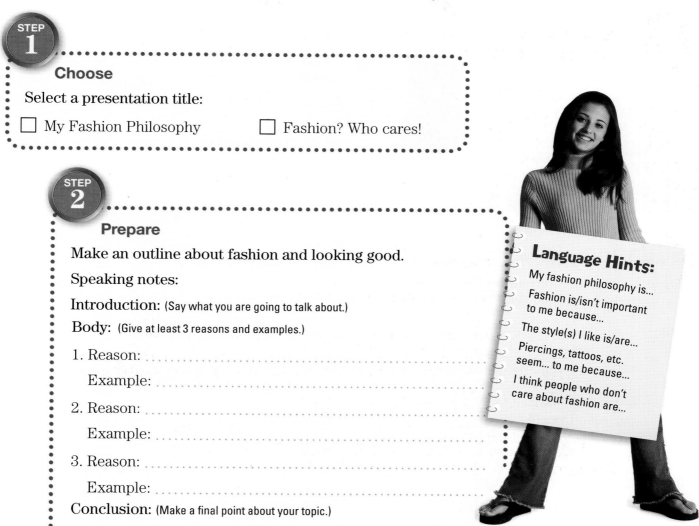

Language Hints:

My fashion philosophy is...

Fashion is/isn't important to me because...

The style(s) I like is/are...

Piercings, tattoos, etc. seem... to me because...

I think people who don't care about fashion are...

STEP 3

Rehearse

Give your presentation to a partner. After practicing once, add more details to your outline.

 Listener task: Ask at least two questions about the things your partner says.

STEP 4

Presentation Tip:
Remember to make eye contact with your audience!

Present

Present to a new partner or to a group. At the end, ask, "Do you have any comments?"

 Listener task: Make a comment about something your partner said. ("You said... I think...")

45

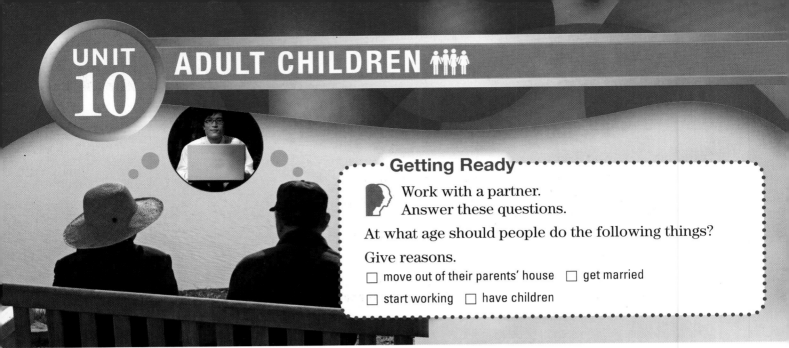

···· **Getting Ready** ···············

Work with a partner.
Answer these questions.

At what age should people do the following things?

Give reasons.

☐ move out of their parents' house   ☐ get married

☐ start working   ☐ have children

Situation

Youth Move is an international talk show about cultural trends. Today's topic is adult children who live with their parents. What do you think about this trend? Listen to the conversation.

Philo: Hello, this is Philo Samra, your host of *Youth Move*. Today's topic is adult children who keep living with their parents. Is this a global phenomenon? Is it a good thing? Today we're talking to Rie Hoshino, a journalist from Tokyo, and Billie Fox, from *Voice* magazine in London. Rie, what's happening in Asia?

Rie: In Japan it's a huge trend. We call adult children living at home "parasite singles."

Philo: Sounds creepy. How about in the UK, Billie?

Billie: Well, something similar is going on here. We call young people who have left home and then return home "boomerang children."

Philo: So are these young people taking advantage of their parents?

Rie: I think they've been spoiled by their parents, so they don't want to grow up. They expect Mommy to cook and clean for them.

Philo: But there must be practical reasons also.

Rie: Of course. Living by yourself costs a lot. Also, families are much smaller than in the past so parents can afford to support their children.

Philo: But that creates problems...

Rie: Well, they get married later, so they don't buy houses, cars, and so on. That's contributing to the bad economy.

Billie: Well, in the UK people see a positive side to all of this.

Philo: For example?

Billie: Well, living at home gives young people a chance to think about their future. They are often quite hard-working. They may be saving to buy their first home.

Philo: But in the past, young people wanted to leave home to be free. What has changed?

Rie: These days society is more materialistic. If they leave home, they will be poorer than now. They want to stay home and keep the high standard of living.

Billie: We shouldn't forget that some parents enjoy having their children at home. Parents and their adult children become more like friends.

Philo: What do our listeners have to say? What are the trends where you live? Our first caller is from New Delhi in India...

Glossary   **trend** = a general direction in which things are moving   **creepy** = disturbing   **spoiled** = selfish, because you always get what you want
materialistic = interested in owning things and having money

••Check Your Understanding ••••••••••••••••••••••••••••••••

Answer the questions. Circle a, b, or c.

1. According to Rie, in Japan, adult children living at home is:
   a) not so common.   b) getting more common.   c) less common than before.

2. In the UK, young people who come back to live with their parents are called:
   a) parasite singles.   b) a huge trend.   c) boomerang children.

3. The criticism of adult children living at home is:
   a) they don't have jobs.   b) they spend too much money.   c) they are selfish.

4. A good thing about adult children living with their parents is:
   a) they have time to think about their future.   b) they give their parents money.

5. One reason why adult children live with their parents is:
   a) the high cost of living.   b) they can't find work.   c) they don't think about their future.

What Do You Think? Track 20

Listen carefully to the opinions of these four people. Who do agree with most? Rank the opinions from 1 to 4 (1 = strongly agree, 4 = strongly disagree).

☐ **Anna:** If adult children keep staying at home, they will never grow up.

☐ **Shingo:** It's important for young people to become independent.

☐ **Mark:** I think it's good for children to stay at home and be close to their parents.

☐ **Iris:** It's really convenient to live at home. I don't blame children for staying.

Discuss your ideas with a partner.
What do you think of the opinions above?

opinion**NETWORK**

I	completely	agree	with Anna.	Don't you?
	strongly			
No way!	I don't	understand	her point at all.	
		get		
Definitely!	She's	100%	right.	
		absolutely		

I strongly agree with Anna. Don't you?

No way! I don't get her point at all. I think it's practical to stay at home.

Extending the Topic *A family crisis*

A Read the problem that Frances has with her son.

My son is 33 years old and not married. He lives with us and doesn't want to live by himself. He has a job, but spends all his money on his hobbies. I cook for him, clean his room, and wash his clothes. I tell him to seriously think about starting his own family, but he says he is just as happy like this and wouldn't change his lifestyle. I'm afraid he will never get married. What should I do?

What advice would you give to Frances?	Check the advice you agree with.	What advice would you give to Frances?	Check the advice you agree with.
Try talking to her son gently.		Stop cleaning his room.	
Make a list of rules.		Stop cooking for him.	
Tell him he must save his money and move out.		Lock the door if he comes home too late.	
My idea:		My idea:	

B Work with two or three classmates. Discuss your advice for Frances.

BASIC

A: Do you think that Frances should try talking to her son gently?

B: I think that's a good idea. He might get angry if she's not gentle.

EXTENSION

A: But what about cleaning his room and cooking for him? I think she should stop.

B: Yeah, me too. She's not his housekeeper.

A: Exactly! He's a grown man. He should really do those things himself.

Report your group's ideas to the class. What is your best advice for Frances?

Extra Activity *Role play*

 Situation: Interview with a son or daughter living with parents.

A: You are an interviewer.

B: You are a 33-year-old son or daughter who doesn't want to move out.

Interviewer, ask B questions about his/her lifestyle. For example: What kind of job do you have?

Practice your role play. Then do your role play interview in front of another pair.

Culture Corner

Success Factors for Boomerang Kids

- The boomerang kid pays rent or contributes to the household in a tangible way.
- The boomerang kid gets along with Mom.
- The return is temporary and a one-time event.
- The parents are in a long-term marriage.
- The return is a safety net while the boomerang kid makes a transition, based on a clear-cut needs.
- The boomerang kid is cheerful and good company.

Source: newyorklife.com

Sharing My Ideas *Milestones*

What kind of family life do you want to have in the future?

Milestones are important dates in life, such as graduation, marriage, having a child, getting a first job, starting a company, etc. Talk about a past milestone, or your hopes for a future milestone.

STEP 1

Choose

Select a milestone:

My milestone ....

This is a ☐ future ☐ past milestone.

Language Hints:

An important milestone for me was (will be)...

At the (ceremony, interview, wedding, etc.) I felt (will feel)...

One thing that happened was...

One thing I hope for is...

This milestone is important because...

STEP 2

Prepare

Make notes. Use the questions to help you. Give your reasons.

Speaking notes:

Introduction: ....

Body: ....

Conclusion: ....

| What milestone did you choose? | How old were you (will you be)? | What other milestones are important to you? |
| Why is it important to you? | How did (will) you feel? | |

STEP 3

Rehearse

Practice with a partner. Try speaking without looking at your notes.

 Listener task: After listening, help your partner add more detail to the outline.

Presentation Tip:
Make sure your notes are brief and organized before you begin your presentation.

STEP 4

Present

Give your presentation to a new partner or to a group. Make eye contact with the listeners.

 Listener task: After listening, ask a question about the speaker's milestone.

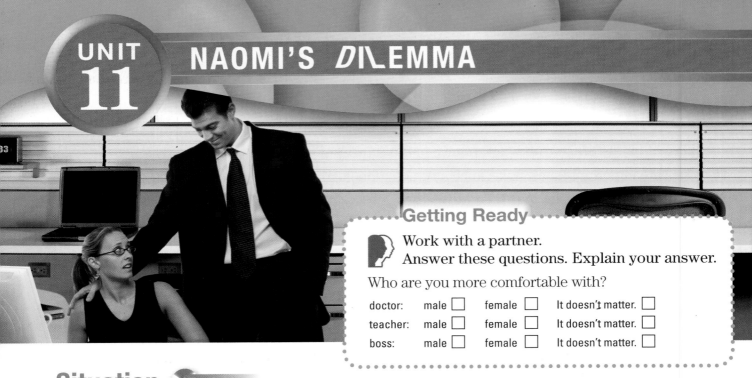

Getting Ready

Work with a partner.
Answer these questions. Explain your answer.

Who are you more comfortable with?

doctor:	male ☐	female ☐	It doesn't matter. ☐
teacher:	male ☐	female ☐	It doesn't matter. ☐
boss:	male ☐	female ☐	It doesn't matter. ☐

Situation Track 21

Naomi calls her older brother, Tom, to ask for advice about a situation at work.
Listen to their conversation.

Tom: Hello.

Naomi: Hey, Tom. It's me.

Tom: Oh, hey, Naomi. What's wrong?

Naomi: I need your advice. I... I have a problem at work.

Tom: Let's hear it.

Naomi: Well, it's... it's my boss.

Tom: What did he do?

Naomi: He's... he's acting weird.

Tom: I thought you liked him.

Naomi: I did, up until yesterday.

Tom: What happened?

Naomi: Well... OK. I had just sent him this long email updating him on a really cool project I was working on. And he called me into his office and I thought he was going to talk about that. But then he asked me out.

Tom: On a date?

Naomi: Yeah. It was really uncomfortable.

Tom: Oh, I get it. So you don't like him that way.

Naomi: I thought he was great, until he did that, you know? Now I don't what to think. It was just so inappropriate. It was creepy.

Tom: Creepy? I mean, is he older than you?

Naomi: No, not really. A few years, maybe.

Tom: Well, I mean, is he married?

Naomi: No.

Tom: Did he act weird with you?

Naomi: No, he did not act weird with me.

Tom: Did he threaten to fire you if you didn't go out with him or something?

Naomi: No, he was actually very polite. But wait, that's not the point. He shouldn't ask me for a date at work like that. It's not right. It's going to mess everything up.

Tom: Naomi, dating nowadays, it's becoming a lot more common in the workplace.

Naomi: Tom, don't you get it? He's my boss! I'm afraid he might fire me if I say no.

Tom: I don't think it'll come to that. Listen, things are really changing nowadays. I'm not sure those old rules apply anymore. And, I mean, you're both adults, and you like each other, so why not give it a shot?

Naomi: I don't know if that's such a good idea. But thanks for your advice anyway.

Tom: Yeah. What are big brothers for?

Glossary   **updating** = giving someone the latest news about something or someone   **inappropriate** = wrong or not proper for the situation
mess everything up = to ruin a situation   **give it a shot** = to try something and see what happens

•• **Check Your Understanding** ••••••••••••••••••••••••••••••••

Answer the questions.

1. What was Naomi expecting when her boss called her into his office?
2. Why did her boss want to talk to her?
3. Why is Naomi so upset about the situation?
4. How did she feel about her boss before yesterday?
5. What is her brother's advice?

What Do You Think? Track 22

A Listen carefully to the opinions of these four people. Check the opinions you agree with.

☐ **Susan:** Naomi should go out with her boss one time. One time won't hurt.

☐ **Ken:** Naomi should find a new job first, and then quit her job.

☐ **Luis:** Naomi should keep quiet. If she complains, she could lose her job.

☐ **Yeon-Suk:** Naomi should refuse politely and tell her boss she has a boyfriend. He will never find out the truth.

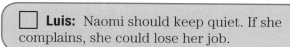

 B Work with a partner.
Share your opinion.

opinion NETWORK

What do you think of	Yeon-Suk's	idea?
	Ken's	opinion?
I think	she makes a good point.	
	he has the right idea.	
Yeah, I	think so, too.	
	totally agree with you.	

What do you think of Susan's idea?

I think she makes a good point.

Yeah, I think so, too. One time won't hurt anything.

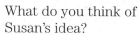

Extending the Topic *Business dinner or date?*

A Naomi and her boss give their points of view about the situation at work. Is Naomi overreacting? What does her boss want? Which ideas do you think are right? Write R (right) or W (wrong).

Boss's Ideas	R or W	Naomi's Ideas	R or W
1. If Naomi wants to get ahead in the company, she will be happy to go out with me for dinner.		1. My boss wants me to be his girlfriend.	
2. It's good for a boss to talk over company business with his employees at dinner after work.		2. If I go to dinner with him, he will think I want to be his girlfriend.	
3. When I take an employee to dinner, it shows him or her that I approve of their work. Then they will work harder!		3. It's not a good idea for a boss and an employee to see each other after work.	
4. I didn't ask her for a date. I just asked her out to dinner.		4. If there are other employees at dinner, it's OK. But going out alone with the boss is uncomfortable.	

B Discuss your ideas with two or three classmates.

BASIC

> A: What do you think Naomi's boss wants?

> B: I'm not sure. Maybe he really does want her to work harder.

EXTENSION

> A: Do you really think so? She seems pretty sure that he wants more than that.

> B: Come on! Bosses have dinner with their employees all the time.

> A: That may be true. But this situation seems a little uncomfortable.

Report your group's ideas to the class. Who believes Naomi? Who believes her boss?

Extra Activity *Role play*

 Situation: A mediator asks Naomi and her boss questions about their situation.

> A: You are a mediator.

> B: You are Naomi.

> C: You are Naomi's boss.

Mediator, ask Naomi and her boss questions about their situation. For example:

(To the boss) • Why did you ask Naomi to go to dinner?
(To Naomi) • How did you feel when your boss asked you to go to dinner with him?

Culture Corner

How to Deal with a Bad Boss

- Make sure you are doing everything right.
- Compile a list of bad boss behaviors.
- Keep a journal of incidents.
- Find a mentor within the company.
- Report your bad boss.
- Don't sacrifice your health or self-esteem.

Source: quintcareers.com

Sharing My Ideas *Sexual harassment*

STEP 1

Choose

Select one of the situations below.

A Mariko has a great job; she really loves her work. But she has a problem with a male co-worker, Kenji. She thinks Kenji likes her. He's always trying to talk to her about her personal life. He's asked her to go out with him, but Mariko has always refused. Now Kenji touches her arm or her shoulder when they are talking. She knows that her boss likes Kenji because he is very smart and a hard worker. What can Mariko do?

B Shen is a history major, and is taking a seminar with one of the most respected professors at his university. It's a small class, with only 12 graduate students. He likes the seminar but is having a problem with the professor. She has asked him to go to coffee with her after class several times. She says she wants to talk about the next assignment with him. Shen doesn't feel comfortable being alone with her. What should Shen do?

STEP 2

Prepare

Think about what Mariko/Shen should do. Give reasons for your ideas. Make an outline of what you will say.

Speaking notes:

Introduction:

Which situation did you select?

Body:

Is this sexual harassment? Why or why not?

What should Mariko/Shen do?

How will it help Mariko/Shen solve the problem?

Conclusion:

Summarize your reasons.

Language Hints:
I chose situation A/B.
I think /I don't think that...
Mariko/Shen should...
This will help her/him because...
To sum up,...

STEP 3

Rehearse

Find a classmate who has the same situation. Present your ideas.

 Listener Task: Is the solution to the problem clear? Tell your partner what you think.

STEP 4

Presentation Tip:
Be a good listener. Pay attention. Take notes during your classmates' presentations.

Present

Present your situation to a new classmate or to a group.

 Listener task: Do you agree with the solution? Why or why not?

Getting Ready

Work with a partner.
Answer these questions.

1. What do you like about your country?

2. What don't you like?

3. Where in the world would you most like to live?

Situation 🔊 Track 23

Dale and Chip are British students studying in Tokyo. They are living in the same dorm, but they've had very different reactions to their time abroad. Listen to their conversation.

Dale: Hi, I'm back!

Chip: Where have you been?

Dale: After class I went through Harajuku to the Meiji Shrine. Amazing! Then I found this noodle restaurant. I talked to the owner. Great fun! What did you do?

Chip: I took a walk and went down to that pub we went to the other day.

Dale: Again? What's wrong with you? We're in Tokyo, man! Why go to a British pub in Asia?

Chip: I don't know. I'm tired of temples and stuff. Everything is too touristy and crowded. I wanted some good food.

Dale: Japanese food is great. And, hey, it's a lot healthier than British food. But you barely even try any.

Chip: I've tried lots of things. I just don't like most of it, that's all.

Dale: But we only have another month on our study abroad program. You have to take advantage of your time here.

Chip: I'm tired of studying Japanese. I guess I'm just tired of all the hassle of being here.

Dale: That's culture shock. You're stressed out because you're in a new culture.

Chip: What new culture? Tokyo is totally modern. It's like big cities everywhere—traffic, too many people. I can't even FIND Japanese culture here.

Dale: Maybe it's because you hardly go out and find it! If you tried a little harder, you might discover some things, like the customs are really different.

Chip: Really? People bow instead of shaking hands, but so what?

Dale: You are so negative. You need to be more open-minded. It's cool here. And Britain is so boring and old-fashioned.

Chip: I'm proud to be English. You should be more proud of your country.

Dale: You think I'm not?

Chip: Sometimes. Sometimes I really think you've gone native, you know.

Dale: All right, let's not argue. Come on, I'll buy you a beer at the pub.

Glossary   **take advantage of** = to get as much as you can from   **hassle** = a minor problems or inconvenience
culture shock = the feeling of stress from being in a new environment   **open-minded** = open to new ideas

Check Your Understanding

Answer the questions.

1. What did Dale do after class?
2. What did Chip do after class?
3. How does Dale feel about his experience in Tokyo?
4. What is Chip's explanation for the way that Dale feels?
5. What does Dale say about Chip's feelings about Britain?

What Do You Think? Track 24

A Listen carefully to the opinions of these four people. Check the opinions that you agree with.

☐ **Mark:** Chip is too narrow-minded. He should appreciate his time abroad.

☐ **Iris:** Dale should appreciate his own country, not just foreign countries.

☐ **Anna:** It's normal to be stressed when we are abroad.

☐ **Shingo:** Chip is right. Having pride in your own country is important.

B Work with a classmate.
Talk about the opinions above.

opinion NETWORK

Do you agree with	Mark's opinion?	
	what Mark says?	
No,	I don't.	It's important to be proud of your country.
	not really.	
	not at all!	
Yes,	I do.	Chip has too much pride in his country.
	I guess so.	
	completely!	

Do you agree with what Mark says?

No, not really. I think it's important to be proud of your country.

Extending the Topic *Country pride questionnaire*

 A How much pride do you have in your country? Circle your answers.

	Absolutely!	Yes.	I guess.	Not really.
My country is very beautiful.	1	2	3	4
The history of my country is interesting.	1	2	3	4
The language(s) spoken in my country is/are beautiful.	1	2	3	4
I like to tell foreigners about my country.	1	2	3	4
I am proud to be from my country.	1	2	3	4

Calculate your score:

5–11 = weak pride	
12–15 = medium pride	
16–20 = strong pride	

Work with a partner. Talk about your score.

A: What was your score?
B: According to this, I have medium pride in my country.
A: Do you think that's true?
B: Yes, I do.

What questions would you add to a country pride questionnaire?

 B Share your results with two or three classmates.

BASIC

A: The questionnaire says, "My country is very beautiful." What do you think about that?

B: Absolutely. One thing that is beautiful is the coastline. The beaches are amazing!

EXTENSION

B: Do you think your country is very beautiful?

A: I guess so. I mean, the architecture is beautiful.

B: That counts!

Share your group's ideas with the class. Who is the biggest patriot (most proud of his/her country) in your group?

Extra Activity *Debate*

 Work in a group of 5.

Pair A: You believe that living in another country helps me understand my country and myself.

Pair B: You believe that living in another country is a waste of time.

First, Pair A and pair B work with your partners. Make a list of your reasons. Then, exchange ideas with the other pair.

The Judge: Which pair made the better argument? Why?

 **Culture Corner**

Stages of Culture Shock

Stage 1—Excitement
- The individual experiences a holiday or "honeymoon" period with their new surroundings.

Stage 2—Withdrawal
- The individual now has some more face-to-face experience of the culture and starts to find things different, strange, and frustrating.

Stage 3—Adjustment
- The individual now has a routine, feels more settled, and is more confident in dealing with the new culture.

Stage 4—Enthusiasm
- The individual now feels "at home."

Source: kwintessential.co.uk

Sharing My Ideas *Tour guide!*

What do you recommend to a foreigner visiting your country and region?

STEP 1

Choose

Select your presentation title:

☐ Places to Go ☐ Things to Try ☐ Things to Learn

☐ ....
(your tour guide topic)

Language Hints:

In the morning/afternoon/evening,...

On the first /second, etc. day,...

You simply must (see, go to, try, etc.)...

One of my favorite things is...

STEP 2

Prepare

Use the chart to make a schedule.

Speaking notes:

Schedule	Place or thing to do	Explanation
Example: Day one	Eiffel Tower	Romantic place. Built more than 100 years ago.

STEP 3

Rehearse

Explain a trip to a partner. Include extra information not written in the chart.

 Listener task: At the end, tell the speaker what you'd like more information about.

Presentation Tip:
You are a tour guide! Show your enthusiasm for the trip!

STEP 4

Present

Present your plan to a new partner or to a group.

 Listener task: At the end, ask a question about the places being explained.

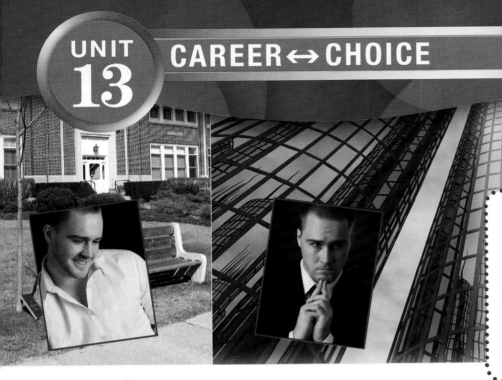

Getting Ready

Work with a partner. Answer these questions.

1. When you were a child, what did you want to be?
2. What is your job now? / What kind of job do you want?
3. How did you/will you choose your career path?

Situation Track 25

Leno has been offered two jobs, but he and his friend Bruce disagree about which one is the better offer. Listen to their conversation.

Leno: So, how's your job search going?

Bruce: Great! You won't believe this—I got a job offer from Promolix! Oh, and one from Ecolene, too.

Leno: Congratulations! That sounds like an easy choice. Promolix is a chemical company. Yuck!

Bruce: So what?

Leno: Well, Ecolene is a dynamic company. It specializes in environmentally friendly products, right? The president's a woman —it's a very progressive company. You can dress casual... Sounds like the perfect job.

Bruce: Actually, I'm thinking about taking the Promolix job.

Leno: You're thinking about taking the Promolix job? You're kidding!

Bruce: Listen, I'd be crazy to say no. It pays a lot more than Ecolene and it's a much bigger company.

Leno: But you'll be a robot in a suit! Is that what you want? The salary may be bigger, but you'll work—what?—70 hours a week!

Bruce: Well, you have to work hard to succeed.

Leno: Maybe, but they make chemicals that are terrible for the environment. Weren't they involved in an illegal dumping scandal?

Bruce: That could happen to any company. Besides, who knows how long a small company like Ecolene will be around? I don't see any advantage to working there.

Leno: Really? Well, less stress is one thing. And they're more socially responsible. I'm sure Ecolene has a more creative work environment—not just competition for the next promotion.

Bruce: Honestly, are you being a bit naive? Business is all about competition. And in a big company you have more room to move up.

Leno: If I were you, I'd take a bit less money and have a better life.

Bruce: To be honest, that sounds a bit lazy to me. I have big dreams. I want to succeed.

Leno: Well, I don't think money and a big office can make someone happy. I think you're making a mistake.

Glossary **dynamic** = full of energy **dumping** = throwing away **scandal** = an event that shocks people in a bad way **socially responsible** = caring about people and the environment **promotion** = a move to a higher position

•• **Check Your Understanding** ••••••••••••••••••

Are the sentences true or false? Circle T, F, or NI (not enough information).

1. Bruce would consider Ecolene if it paid more money.   T / F / NI
2. Leno thinks that Bruce should choose a company with a good work environment.   T / F / NI
3. Bruce doesn't mind working in a competitive environment.   T / F / NI
4. Bruce and Leno agree about what success is.   T / F / NI
5. Bruce and Leno agree about which job offer is better.   T / F / NI

What Do You Think? Track 26

 A Listen carefully to the opinions of these four people. Check all of the opinions that you agree with.

☐ **Ken:** You shouldn't sell yourself to whatever company pays the most. Lifestyle is important, too.

☐ **Susan:** If you want success, you have to work hard and put up with stress.

☐ **Luis:** Leno's right about money. You can't buy happiness with it.

☐ **Yeon-Suk:** Leno's not being realistic. Bruce should take the job that pays more.

B   What do you think of the opinions above? Share your ideas with a classmate.

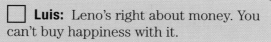 **opinionNETWORK**

I think	Ken	has the best argument.
		has the right idea.
What	do you think?	
	is your opinion?	
If you ask me,	his argument is a bit weak.	
	his idea doesn't make sense.	

I think Ken has the right idea. What do you think?

If you ask me, his argument is a bit weak. Salary is important, too.

Extending the Topic *What's important when choosing a job?*

A Rank the following job characteristics. Which is most important to you?
1 = really important, 2/3 = pretty important, 4/5 = not too important, 6 = unimportant

☐ the size of the company	☐ relaxed work environment
☐ good benefits	☐ high salary
☐ creative work	☐ famous company
☐ easy commute	☐ high-status job
☐ flexible hours	☐ chance to move ahead
☐ chance to travel	

B Discuss your ranking with two or three classmates. Explain your choices.

BASIC

A: What ranking did you give the size of the company?

B: I gave it a 5. I don't think that's important compared to other things.

EXTENSION

A: Why's that?

B: I think that the type of job is more important than the size of the company.

A: Yeah. I guess I agree with that.

Report your group's ideas to the class.
What are the most important job characteristics in your group?

Extra Activity *Role play*

Situation: A fourth-year university student is interested in getting a job at the company where his/her friend works.

A: You are a university student.

B: You are the student's friend.

Student A, ask your friend questions about his/her job. For example:

• How big is your company?
• What kind of benefits do you have?
• Can you do creative work?

 **Culture Corner**

Tips for Job Interviews

• Be early.
• Learn the name of your interviewer.
• Use good manners with everyone you meet.
• Relax and answer each question concisely.
• Be cooperative and enthusiastic.
• Ask questions about the position and the organization, but avoid questions whose answers can easily be found on the company website.
• Also, avoid asking questions about salary and benefits unless a job offer is made.
• Thank the interviewer when you leave.
• Send a short thank-you note.

Source: bls.gov

Sharing My Ideas *Job interview—presenting yourself*

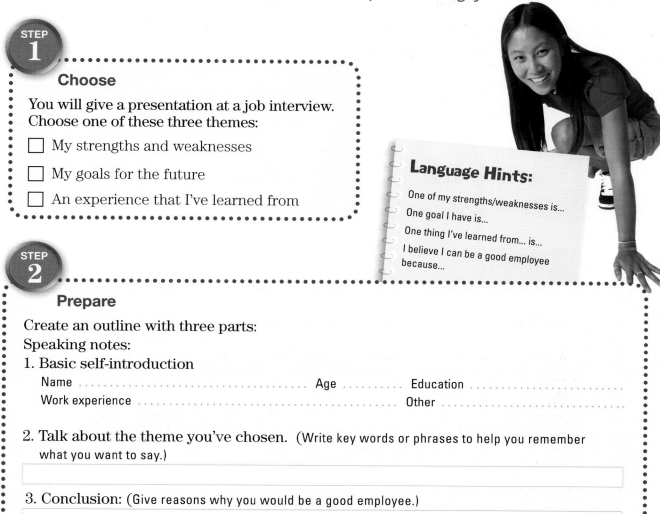

STEP 1

Choose

You will give a presentation at a job interview. Choose one of these three themes:

☐ My strengths and weaknesses

☐ My goals for the future

☐ An experience that I've learned from

Language Hints:

One of my strengths/weaknesses is...

One goal I have is...

One thing I've learned from... is...

I believe I can be a good employee because...

STEP 2

Prepare

Create an outline with three parts:
Speaking notes:

1. Basic self-introduction

Name .... Age .... Education ....

Work experience .... Other ....

2. Talk about the theme you've chosen. (Write key words or phrases to help you remember what you want to say.)

3. Conclusion: (Give reasons why you would be a good employee.)

STEP 3

Rehearse

Practice giving your presentation to a partner. Afterward, ask, "How can I improve my presentation?"

Listener task: Do you understand your partner's reasons? Should he/she explain more?

STEP 4

Present

Give your presentation to a new partner or to a group.

Listener task: You are the employer. Ask two questions about the presenter and his/her experiences.

Presentation Tip:
You want the job! Act positive and outgoing.

Getting Ready

Work with a partner.
Answer these questions.

1. Do people from other countries live in your country?

2. What countries do they come from?

3. Discuss your answers with a classmate.

Situation

Track 27

This is a magazine article. What does the author think is happening in his country, Shingistan?
Listen to the article.

Our Country Magazine

Save Our Beloved Nation, Shingistan!

B. A. Ware

Wake up, fellow citizens of Shingistan! Wake up and look around you! What do you see? Who do you see? Take a good look. How many people do you see who were not born here?

I am afraid that our beloved country is in trouble, serious trouble. We have a wonderful country with a glorious past. We have been in many wars and each time we have won. But this war is different, and I am afraid that we are losing.

The enemy walks freely among us. The enemy does not carry guns and does not attack us. But the enemy will soon take over our country without firing a single shot. And this will happen because we are not aware of the enemy. We are not aware that we are at war.

The enemy is the people who do not belong here. There are too many immigrants from Kushtonya and I feel that the Kushtos are taking over our country. You can easily see them. They are very different from us. They have different-colored skin, eyes, and hair.

We let the Kushtos come into our country to work. They do the work that we do not want to do. They work on our farms and in our factories. They clean up our cities and build our roads and our houses. They do these jobs because they are not very smart. And they are lazy. But they work for very little money.

The enemy has a very different religion from us. They believe in a different god. Moreover, they speak a different language. They are not smart enough to learn our wonderful language, Shingistani.

Our laws allow them to become citizens of our country. They vote in our elections. They have large families. Soon there will be more of them than us. They will take over our country.

Wake up! Look around you! We must change our laws to save our country. We have to send the Kushtos back to Kushtonya.

Glossary **citizens** = legal residents or people of a country   **immigrant** = person who moves permanently to a new country
vote = to choose somebody or something (in an election)   **election** = event at which somebody is chosen for public office by vote

• • **Check Your Understanding** •

Answer the questions.

1. How are the Kushtos different from the people of Shingistan?

2. What kind of work do the Kushtos do in Shingistan?

3. According to B. A. Ware, why do they do this work?

4. Why does Mr. Ware think the Kushtos are dangerous to his country?

5. What does Mr. Ware want to do to save his country?

What Do You Think? Track 28

 A   Listen carefully to the opinions of these four people. Who do you agree with most? Rate the opinions from 1 to 4 (1 = strongly agree, 4 = strongly disagree).

Shingo: Mr. Ware is a good person. He wants to save his country.

Iris: Mr. Ware is a racist. He believes that a person's physical appearance—a person's race—shows intelligence.

Anna: Humans can be divided into different races. Maybe some races are better than other races.

Mark: There is no scientific evidence for human races. People who use race to judge people are prejudiced.

 B   Work with a partner.
Discuss the opinions above.

What do you think of Shingo's opinion?

To be honest, I think he's right. Too many immigrants can hurt a country.

opinion**NETWORK**

What do you think of	Shingo's opinion?	
How do you feel about		
To tell the truth,	I agree with him.	It's important to be proud of your country.
To be honest,	I think he's right.	
I	completely	disagree with him.
	totally	

Really? I totally disagree with him. The immigrants in this country work hard.

Extending the Topic *Immigrant jobs*

 A What jobs do immigrants do in your country? Add your own ideas.

Job	Yes	No	I'm not sure	Job	Yes	No	I'm not sure
doctor				store clerk			
bus driver				computer programmer			
taxi driver				politician			
restaurant worker				nurse			
teacher				construction worker			
my idea:				my idea:			

 B Talk about your ideas with two or three classmates. Then answer one of these questions:

- What are the advantages and disadvantages of different races living in one country?
- Is diversity a strength or a weakness for a country?
- Should immigrants speak the new language and adapt to the country's customs and cultures?
- Should they keep their languages and cultures?

BASIC

A: What jobs do immigrants do in ....?

B: Most of the immigrants are restaurant workers and store clerks.

EXTENSION

A: So, do you think diversity is a strength or a weakness?

B: I guess it's a strength. It makes people learn to accept each other.

A: Do you really think so? I'm not sure about that.

Report your group's ideas to the class. According to your group, which things should the government control? Not control?

Extra Activity *Debate*

Work in groups of 5.

Pair A: You believe that immigrants are good for a country.
Pair B: You believe that immigrants are not good for a country.
The Judge: You will listen to their reasons.

First, Pair A and Pair B prepare your reasons. Then, exchange ideas with the other pair.

The Judge: Which pair made the better argument?

Culture Corner

Number of Immigrants Around the World

1. United States	38,355,000
2. Russia	12,080,000
3. Germany	10,144,000
4. Ukraine	6,833,000
5. France	6,471,000
6. Saudi Arabia	6,361,000
7. Canada	6,106,000
8. India	5,700,000
9. United Kingdom	5,408,000
10. Spain	4,790,000

Source: wikipedia.org

Sharing My Ideas *The rights of immigrants*

First, think about the rights of citizens of your country, such as owning property, going to school, having a driver's license, and voting. Make a list. Now think about immigrants who do not have citizenship. Do they have the same rights as citizens? Can they do the same things as citizens?

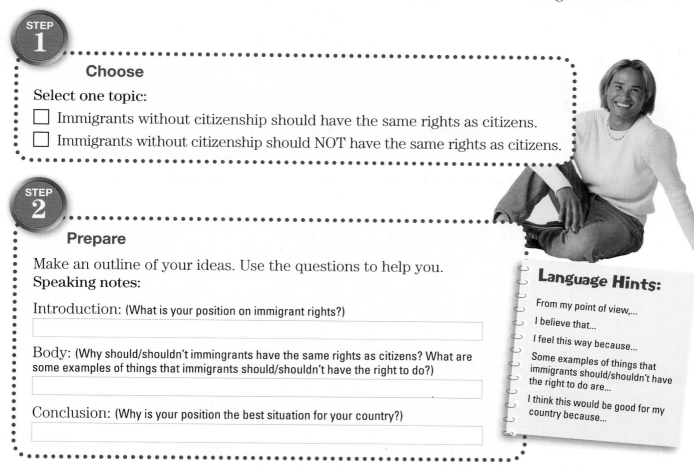

STEP 1

Choose

Select one topic:

☐ Immigrants without citizenship should have the same rights as citizens.

☐ Immigrants without citizenship should NOT have the same rights as citizens.

STEP 2

Prepare

Make an outline of your ideas. Use the questions to help you.
Speaking notes:

Introduction: (What is your position on immigrant rights?)

Body: (Why should/shouldn't immingrants have the same rights as citizens? What are some examples of things that immigrants should/shouldn't have the right to do?)

Conclusion: (Why is your position the best situation for your country?)

Language Hints:

From my point of view,...

I believe that...

I feel this way because...

Some examples of things that immigrants should/shouldn't have the right to do are...

I think this would be good for my country because...

STEP 3

Rehearse

Practice with a classmate.

 Listener task:
Does your partner give enough examples? Help your partner improve his/her outline.

STEP 4

Presentation Tip:
Write brief notes in your outline. Don't write out complete sentences.

Present

Present your ideas to a new partner or to a group.

 Listener task: Do you agree with the speaker's position? Write one question you would like to ask the speaker: "I disagree with… Could you explain… ? OR "I agree with you on…, but I have one question… "

Situation Track 29

Trin loves computers and technology, but Ann-Li thinks they get in the way of their relationship. Listen to their conversation.

Ann-Li: Honey...

Trin: Wait a second. I'm setting up this new network.

Ann-Li: Oh no, not again.

Trin: What's wrong?

Ann-Li: Trin, you spend all of your time at the computer or with your high-tech toys.

Trin: But this is great! Our computer will control the temperature in the house, and turn off all the lights automatically!

Ann-Li: Listen to me! I don't need a computer to tell me when I'm cold. And I've got hands to turn off the lights.

Trin: But...

Ann-Li: Let's turn off your computer and have a nice dinner tonight. We'll take a stroll, and then we'll snuggle up on the sofa, and put on a CD.

Trin: Oh, I've put them into my computerized music system.

Ann-Li: Stop it! Let's spend some time together. Look, we hardly ever go out. You say it's too much trouble. Instead of going to see a movie you just want to download it from the Internet.

Trin: It's so much simpler.

Ann-Li: But, honey, life isn't just about convenience. And we never talk anymore.

Trin: Never talk? But I talk to you.

Ann-Li: Yeah! You tell me about software... online gaming characters... your virtual world.

Trin: That's what I'm interested in.

Ann-Li: But it's not real! If you live your life online, the important things will pass you by. Don't you remember what day it is today?

Trin: Today? Uh, Tuesday? Wait, let me look at my calendar online. Oh!

Ann-Li: Yes...

Trin: It's our anniversary today.

Ann-Li: You see?

Trin: Oh, you're right. Sorry, I forgot. I'll have to put that into my important dates file.

Ann-Li: You're impossible!

·· Check Your Understanding ····················

Answer the questions. Circle a, b, or c.

1. Why does Ann-Li say, "Oh no, not again."?

   a) Trin forgot their anniversary again. b) Trin often has high-tech projects. c) Trin broke the computer again.

2. What does Ann-Li think about Trin's new project?

   a) She thinks it's too expensive. b) She thinks it's a good idea. c) She thinks it's unnecessary.

3. Why don't Ann-Li and Trin go out very often?

   a) Trin prefers to stay home. b) Ann-Li doesn't want to. c) Neither of them likes going out very much.

4. What did Trin forget?

   a) Ann-Li's birthday b) their anniversary c) the day of the week

5. Why does Ann-Li say, "You're impossible!" at the end?

   a) Trin doesn't understand the problem. b) Trin always makes promises he doesn't keep. c) Trin didn't tell Ann-Li the truth.

What Do You Think? Track 30

A

Listen carefully to the opinions of these four people.
Check the opinions you agree with.

☐ **Susan:** Trin and Ann-Li have problems in their relationship, but it's not technology's fault.

☐ **Ken:** These days, a lot of people spend too much time using computers.

☐ **Yeon-Suk:** Technology makes people forget the simple pleasures in life.

☐ **Luis:** Ann-Li should be more understanding of Trin's interests!

B

Work with a classmate.
Share your opinions.

opinion NETWORK

Whose opinion	do you	agree with the most?
		least agree with?
Definitely Susan's. She	really knows	what she's talking about.
	doesn't know	
Probably Luis's. He	has	the right idea.
	doesn't have	a clue.

Whose opinion do you agree with the most?

Probably Ken's. I think he's right. Trin needs to communicate better. What do you think?

I think he's letting his hobby control his life.

Extending the Topic *High-tech lifestyle*

Interview a partner to see if they have a "high-tech lifestyle." Ask the questions and mark the answers.

Do you...	Yes	No	Do you...	Yes	No
have a computer?	☐	☐	like new high-tech things?	☐	☐
have a cell phone?	☐	☐	search for information on the Internet?	☐	☐
send text messages?	☐	☐	have a personal Web page?	☐	☐
often go online?	☐	☐	have online friends?	☐	☐
play online games?	☐	☐	have a digital music player?	☐	☐
shop online?	☐	☐	have a blog?	☐	☐

Calculate the results. Number of "yes" answers:
0 - 3 = very low-tech lifestyle   4 - 6 = low-tech lifestyle   7 - 9 = high-tech lifestyle   10 - 12 = very high-tech lifestyle

B Share your results.

BASIC

A: What's your result?

B: 8. So that means I have a high-tech lifestyle.

EXTENSION

A: Do you agree with your result?

B: Yeah. I guess I'm a pretty high-tech person.

A: What's your favorite high-tech gadget?

B: Oh. I'm not sure. I have so many!

Report your group's ideas to the class. Who has the most high-tech lifestyle? Least high-tech?

Extra Activity *Debate*

 Work in groups of 5.

Pair A: You believe that high-tech toys improve the quality of our lives.
Pair B: You believe that high-tech toys do NOT improve the quality of our lives.
The Judge: You will listen to their reasons.

First, Pair A and Pair B prepare your reasons.
Then, exchange ideas with the other pair.

The Judge: Which pair made the better argument? Why?

 **Culture Corner**

High-tech Toys

How much time do some anime fans spend on the Internet?

Poll Results (Voters: 568): How Many Hours a Week?

Less than 5 hours	36 voters	6.34%
5 - 15	75	13.20%
16 - 25	102	17.96%
26 - 35	62	10.92%
More than 35 hours	293	51.58%

Source: hongfire.com

Sharing My Ideas *Then and now*

Make a presentation comparing the past and the present.

STEP 1

Choose

Select your theme:

☐ My grandparents and me   ☐ Technology then and now

☐ My childhood days and now   My idea ....

Language Hints:

In the past,...

These days,...

One thing that has changed is...

...was better/worse in the past because...

I would/wouldn't like life in the past because...

An advantage to modern life is...

STEP 2

Prepare

Make an outline.

Introduction: Today, I will talk about...

| |
| |

| Before,... | Now,... |
| | |

Conclusion: My conclusion about life in the past and now is that...

| |

STEP 3

Rehearse

Practice giving your presentation to a partner. Afterward, add more details to your outline.

 Listener task: After listening, tell your partner which part of the presentation needs more detail.

STEP 4

Present

Present to a new classmate or to a group.

 Listener task: Tell the speaker if you agree with his/her conclusion.

Presentation Tip:
Use hand gestures when you make comparisons.

UNIT 16 A WOMAN'S PLACE

Getting Ready

Work with a partner.
Answer these questions.

1. When you were young, did your mother work outside the home?

2. In your country, do most mothers work or stay at home with the children?

Situation Track 31

The main story in the magazine *Today's Society* is an interview with Dr. Mary Lee. She wrote a book, A *Woman's Place*, which has some controversial ideas about the role of women in society. Listen to the interview.

Today's Society: Dr. Lee, I just finished reading your new book, *A Woman's Place*. You really have some controversial ideas. Could you tell our audience about some of your beliefs?

Dr. Lee: Yes. However, before I do, I want to say that my ideas are based on facts. The facts come from the history of humans all over the world.

Today's Society: OK, I understand. Please tell us some of these facts.

Dr. Lee: First, as we know, a woman's role in many societies is changing. Women want to do what men have done throughout history. Second, this means that the natural order is changing. This has caused many societal problems.

Today's Society: So what do you mean that the natural order is changing?

Dr. Lee: I mean there are changes in the roles and responsibilities of men and women. Nowadays, what women do in society—their roles and responsibilities—has changed a great deal in the past 60 years. Women in many societies no longer stay at home and take care of children. They want to do what men have traditionally done. They want to work outside the home. They want to become leaders.

Today's Society: So why is this causing many problems?

Dr. Lee: Women no longer have the time to take care of their children. In today's world, children grow up and have many problems. They drop out of school, they take drugs, they steal. Today's children are lazy and confused. They need the guidance, love, and support that only mothers who are in the home can give. Women should return to raising and educating children. They are naturally suited to do so. Men should continue to have the main responsibility for earning money for the family. We know from history that men are leaders and women raise children.

Today's Society: You are a woman. Do you think other women agree with you?

Dr. Lee: Many women agree with me. However, some think my idea is old-fashioned, or out-of-date. But it is the one that fits with the natural order.

Glossary **controversial** = causing strong disagreement or disapproval **role** = their position, what they are expected to do
responsibilities = duties **guidance** = help and advice **raising** = bringing up **suited** = fit for **out-of-date** = no longer useful or effective

Check Your Understanding

Answer the questions.

1. What does Dr. Lee say about her ideas?
   a) They are just her opinions.   b) They come from historical facts.   c) They are not controversial.

2. What does Dr. Lee mean by "the natural order"?
   a) The way that nature intends.   b) The way that societies are organized.   c) The way that is best for children.

3. According to Dr. Lee, which of these are the result of mothers not staying at home to raise their children?
   ☐ Children drop out of school.   ☐ They take drugs.   ☐ They take part-time jobs.

4. According to Dr. Lee, why should mothers stay home and raise their children?
   a) That way is best for children's happiness.   b) That way is best for society.   c) That way is best for family stability.

5. According to Dr. Lee, what is the role of men in society?
   a) To work outside the home.   b) To help raise the children.   c) Both a and b.

What Do You Think? Track 32

A Listen carefully to the opinions of these four people. Which person makes the strongest point? Rate the opinions from 1 to 4 (1 = strongest point, 4 = weakest point).

☐ **Iris:** Women are naturally good at raising children and housekeeping.

☐ **Mark:** In today's world, both the husband and the wife need jobs to support a family.

☐ **Shingo:** If women stayed home, society would be better.

☐ **Anna:** It's important for women to have independence. Working outside the home is a good thing.

B Work with a partner.
Talk about your opinion.

How do you feel about Mark's opinion?

opinion NETWORK

How do you feel about			Mark's opinion? / what Mark says?
I	understand	what	he's saying.
I	know		he means.
I	don't believe	he's right.	
	don't think		

I know what he means. Raising a family is expensive these days.

Extending the Topic *Societal roles*

 A Here are some of Dr. Lee's ideas. For each of them, state an opposite or different idea.

Dr. Lee's ideas	Opposite or different ideas
Societies are in trouble because women have jobs outside the home.	Men have caused much of society's problems because most leaders are men.
Women are naturally suited to raising children.	
Men are natural leaders.	
A man's place is outside the home, working to support the family.	
Today's children are lazy and confused because their mothers are working outside of the home.	
Children need the help, love, and support that only mothers who are in the home can give.	

 B Discuss Dr. Lee's ideas with two or three classmates. Give reasons and examples.

BASIC

> A: Dr. Lee says societies are in trouble because women have jobs outside the home. Can you think of an opposite idea?

> B: Sure. Men have caused much of society's problems because most leaders are men.

EXTENSION

> A: Can you give some examples?

> B: Well, there's poverty and homelessness. And what about all of the wars?

> A: Right. I see your point.

Report your group's ideas to the class.
What were some of your group's best opposing ideas?

Extra Activity *Debate*

Work with a partner.

> A: Traditional roles for men and women are unfair!

> B: There's nothing wrong with traditional roles for men and women.

Make notes to prepare. Think about how your partner will respond.
Discuss your opinions with your partner. After you are finished, decide who had stronger arguments.

 **Culture Corner**

Surprise! Men Do Just as Much Work as Women Do

("Work" here means "work for pay" plus "housework and child care.")

- **the US:** Men work an average of 7.9 hours per day, while women also work an average of 7.9 hours per day.

- **Sweden, Norway, and the Netherlands:** Men work more than women, although the differences are small.

- **Belgium, Denmark, Finland, and the UK:** Women work slightly more, though less than 5 percent.

- **Italy:** Women work 8 hours, while men work only 6.5.

- **France:** Women work 7.2 hours and men 6.6.

Source: *The Dismal Science: The Search for Better Economic Policy*

Sharing My Ideas *The ideal spouse*

STEP 1

Choose

Select your title:

☐ My Ideal Wife

☐ My Ideal Husband

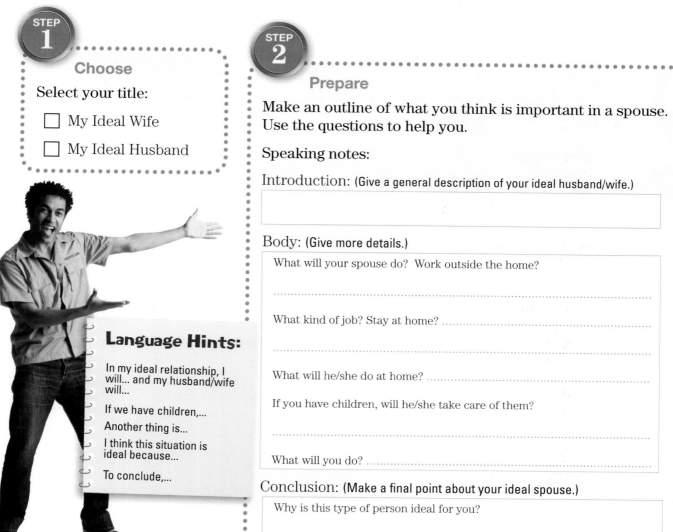

Language Hints:

In my ideal relationship, I will... and my husband/wife will...

If we have children,...

Another thing is...

I think this situation is ideal because...

To conclude,...

STEP 2

Prepare

Make an outline of what you think is important in a spouse. Use the questions to help you.

Speaking notes:

Introduction: (Give a general description of your ideal husband/wife.)

Body: (Give more details.)

What will your spouse do? Work outside the home?

....

What kind of job? Stay at home? ....

....

What will he/she do at home? ....

If you have children, will he/she take care of them?

....

What will you do? ....

Conclusion: (Make a final point about your ideal spouse.)

Why is this type of person ideal for you?

STEP 3

Rehearse

Practice your presentation with a classmate.

 Listener task: Did your partner talk about work, children, and household tasks? Help your partner fill in any missing details.

Presentation Tip:
Don't look at your outline too much. Remember to look at your audience.

STEP 4

Present

Present your ideal spouse to a new partner or to a group.

 Listener task: What was the speaker's conclusion? Why is this the ideal spouse?

Situation Track 33

Sam and Cheryl are newlyweds. Each is having lunch separately with a parent to talk about their marriage. How is their marriage going? Listen to their conversations.

Father: Hey, Cheryl. Thanks for meeting me for lunch. We haven't talked for a while. How are things going?

Cheryl: Well actually, Dad, I need to talk to you. I'm very worried about Sam.

Father: Sam? Is he OK?

Cheryl: Yes... Well, no. It's just that Sam isn't like you, Dad.

Father: Of course not. What do you mean?

Cheryl: I don't know how to say this. He's such a klutz.

Father: A klutz? Really? I mean... I think Sam's a really clever guy.

Cheryl: Well, he's intelligent, but he can't do things around the house. You know our house. It's old. It needs a lot of work and I just assumed that Sam knew how to fix things. He can't even change a light bulb. It's such a disaster! You know how to fix things and build things. Why can't he?

Father: Well, Cheryl, not all guys are good at that kind of stuff. You know, maybe YOU should learn to fix things. Ever thought of that? You're my daughter and I'm sure there are a lot of things you could fix in your house.

Cheryl: Come on, Dad. I can't fix things. That's a man's job.

(Meanwhile, Sam and his mother are having lunch at a different restaurant.)

Mother: Sam, I'm so glad that we could get together for lunch. You sounded worried on the phone. Is every thing OK?

Sam: Well, it's Cheryl. She's terrific and everything. I mean, I love her more and more.

Mother: Then what's the problem?

Sam: She can't cook.

Mother: What? She can't cook?

Sam: Please don't laugh at me, Mom. I'm serious. She cannot cook.

Mother: So what? Lots of people can't cook.

Sam: No, I don't mean, "can't cook." I mean, she really can't cook. She tries, but she can't even cook rice, and she tries to make these special dishes, but they're just terrible. I can't eat them. They're nothing at all like yours. You're such a great cook.

Mother: Well, maybe it's just that you have to get used to her style and maybe YOU should learn to cook. Ever thought of that? You're my son and I'm sure you could be a great cook.

Sam: Me? Cook? Come on, Mom. That's a woman's job.

Glossary **klutz** = a clumsy, awkward person   **disaster** = a terrible situation   **assume** = believe something to be true without thinking about it
compromise = an agreement achieved after everyone involved accepts less than what they wanted

Check Your Understanding

Answer the questions.

1. Why does Cheryl think Sam is a klutz?

2. What compromise does Cheryl's father suggest?

3. What is Sam's problem with Cheryl?

4. What compromise does Sam's mother suggest?

5. What ideas do Sam and Cheryl have about male and female roles in the household?

What Do You Think? Track 34

 Listen carefully to the opinions of these four people. Who has the best idea? Rate their opinions from 1 to 4 (1 = best idea, 4 = worst idea).

Yeon-Suk: Cheryl should learn to fix things and Sam should learn to cook. This is a good compromise.

Luis: If Cheryl and Sam aren't willing to compromise, they should get divorced.

Ken: Cheryl and Sam should have discussed this before they were married. Too late to solve it now.

Susan: They should just accept each other the way they are. That's a good compromise.

  Discuss the opinions with a partner.

opinion NETWORK

I think	Susan's	idea makes the most sense.
I feel		argument is the best.
Yeah,	I think so too.	
	she's got the right idea	
I	don't think so.	
	don't think that makes sense.	

I think Susan's idea makes the most sense.

Yeah, she's got the right idea. It's best to just accept each other.

Extending the Topic *Who is right?*

Think of a compromise for each situation.

Husband	Wife	Compromise
1. wants to get a dog	wants no pets	
2. wants to stay home and watch movies on weekends	wants her husband to go out with her on weekends (movies, dinner, dancing)	
3. wants no children	wants two children	
4. wants to save money for retirement	wants to spend money to enjoy life now	
5. wants to live in the country	wants to live in the city	
my idea:	my idea:	

Discuss your ideas with two or three classmates. Explain your answers.

BASIC

A: What do you think they should do in the first situation?

B: I think that depends on where they live.

EXTENSION

A: What do you mean?

B: Well, if they live in a small apartment, I think they should get a different kind of pet, one that's easy to take care of.

A: Yeah. I guess that might work.

Report your group's ideas to the class. Was it easy or difficult to think of a compromise?

Extra Activity *Role play*

Situation: Interview with Sam/Cheryl.

A: You are an interviewer.
B: You are Cheryl (female students) or Sam (male students).

Interviewer, ask B questions about their situation.
For example:
• Don't you think your ideas about husband/wife roles are a little old-fashioned? Why or why not?

• What are some other ways that you could compromise?

Practice your role play.
Then do your role play in front of another pair.

Culture Corner

Ten Tips for a Happy Marriage

1. Instead of trying to change something he or she does—change yourself!
2. Communication is a key ingredient to any successful marriage.
3. Keep intimacy as a part of the marriage.
4. Accept the flaws in your spouse.
5. Learn to ignore the small stuff.
6. Make sure you choose your battles wisely.
7. Time for friends is also crucial.
8. Never take your spouse for granted.
9. Date—just because you are now legally married, you should not stop dating.
10. Be forgiving with your partner.

Source: families.com

Sharing My Ideas *Making a compromise*

STEP 1

Choose

Read the situations. Select either A or B.

A Yao has moved out of her apartment into a new house. The owner of the apartment says that Yao's apartment has rats in it. He says that Yao did not keep the apartment clean, and that attracted the rats. Yao says there are rats in the world, and that's just part of life. The owner wants Yao to pay to get rid of the rats. Yao refuses to do this.

B Sang-Ki bought a new car but it has many problems. He has returned it to the car dealer from whom he bought the car to get it fixed. The car dealer told him that it will cost a lot of money to fix it. Sang-Ki does not want to pay to get his new car fixed. He says the car dealer should pay to fix it. The car dealer refuses to do this. He says the car belongs to Sang-Ki and Sang-Ki should pay.

STEP 2

Prepare

Think of a compromise for the situation. Make an outline of your ideas. Remember that often in a compromise, no one wins. Both parties often are not happy, but accept the compromise to end the problem.

Speaking notes:

Introduction:

(Briefly state the problem. Present both sides. What is the best compromise?)

[ ]

Body: (How will the compromise work? Why should both parties accept it?)

[ ]

Conclusion: (Why is your compromise a good one?)

[ ]

Language Hints:

Here's the situation.

I think the best way to compromise is...

Let me explain how this will work...

I think both people will accept this compromise because...

Useful vocabulary: fair, accept, right or wrong

STEP 3

Rehearse

Find a classmate who chose the same problem. Listen to your classmate's compromise.

Listener task: Do you understand how the compromise will work? Help your classmate fill in any missing details.

Presentation Tip: Remember to relax and smile!

STEP 4

Present

Present your compromise to a classmate who chose a different situation.

Listener task: Is the compromise fair? Why or why not?

Getting Ready

Work with a partner.
Answer these questions.

1. Do you follow news about wars around the world?

2. Is war an important topic for you to learn about?

3. Can regular people do anything to stop wars?

Situation Track 35

Mir is a teenager who lives in a war zone. On his blog, he is against war and violence, but this creates problems and he faces difficult choices. Listen to his blog entry.

Life is hard in a war zone. I live near the border of my country and there has recently been fighting nearby. My school is often closed and I can't go to see my friends. It's terrible. I have seen dead bodies and destroyed buildings. My uncle was killed by a bomb and my brother is in the army. Many people have left the area. All of these things have made me think a lot about violence and war.

I believe that peace is our most fundamental human right. I am against the war. But my father tells me I am naive. He says that bad people do terrible things. He believes that war is sometimes *Is violence the answer?* necessary to have freedom and real peace. He says the enemy is trying to take what naturally belongs to our country.

But is violence ever the answer? If we become violent, then we become bad, too! Can't we resist injustice without violence?

My father asks me to imagine that a bully is hitting my little sister. Wouldn't I defend her? Of course I would, I say. If we do nothing, he says, we lose everything, including our dignity. He says that some things are worth defending with our lives, but I'm not so sure. The violence I see makes no sense. Houses are bombed. Many people die. War is a nightmare. My father tells me that my doubts are childish. Perhaps he's right.

Soon I will be old enough to fight in this war. I may be forced to join the army. What should I do then? I don't want to fight. My father would be ashamed to hear me say that. If I run away, I can lose everything. If I fight, I may lose everything, too. What should I do? I sometimes feel that I am at war with myself.

Glossary   **human right** = something everybody should absolutely have   **injustice** = unfair treatment of somebody
bully = to be cruel and mean to someone who is weaker   **dignity** = a sense of pride and self-respect   **ashamed** = feeling dishonored and embarrassed

•• Check Your Understanding •••••••••••••••••••••••••••

Answer the questions. Circle a, b, or c.

1. Why has Mir been thinking about violence?
   a) His father talked to him about the war.   b) He has experienced life in a war zone.   c) He may have to join the army.

2. How does Mir's father feel about the war?
   a) He supports the war.   b) He isn't sure what to believe.   c) He is against the war.

3. What does Mir think about violence?
   a) Using it makes people bad.   b) It's part of human nature.   c) It's necessary.

4. How does Mir's father feel about violence?
   a) Sometimes it's necessary.   b) It's unfair.   c) It's the only way to create peace.

5. What will Mir do if he is forced to join the army?
   a) He will run away.   b) He will fight.   c) He's not sure.

naive
bully
dignity
nightmare

What Do You Think? Track 36

Listen to the opinions of these four people.
Check the opinions you agree with.

☐ **Mark:** Mir shouldn't join the army if he doesn't believe in war.

☐ **Shingo:** Mir's father is right. Mir should listen to him.

☐ **Anna:** War will never stop until young people like Mir speak up more.

☐ **Iris:** Mir is a victim of war. He and his family should leave the war zone.

What do you think of the opinions above?
Tell your partner.

opinionNETWORK

I think	Iris	is right.
		is wrong.
Who	do you	agree with?
		think is right?
I	am not sure.	
	really don't know.	
	need to think about it.	

I think Iris is right. Who do you agree with?

I'm not sure.

Extending the Topic *War and peace—my philosophy*

A How do you feel about these statements? Mark 1 = yes, 2 = I'm not sure, 3 = no

☐ It's OK to use violence to defend yourself or your country.

☐ Not enough people care about peace.

☐ War is acceptable if the cause is just.

☐ War and violence are a normal part of being human.

☐ Even reasonable people sometimes become violent.

☐ Violence is always wrong.

☐ As long as humans keep producing deadly weapons, there will be wars.

☐ If all countries owned nuclear weapons, there would be no war.

☐ Peace will be gained by educating children.

☐ There will be another world war someday.

☐ If women became leaders, the world would be more peaceful.

B Share your answers with two or three classmates.

BASIC

A: Do you think it's OK to use violence to defend yourself?

B: No. I think violence makes people more violent.

EXTENSION

A: What do you mean?

B: Well, every time a person responds to violence with violence, they are creating more violent behavior in the world. It doesn't solve anything.

A: Hmm. I'm not sure I see your point.

Report your group's ideas to the class. Which points did you agree on? Which did you disagree on?

Extra Activity *Debate*

Work in groups of 5.

Pair A: You believe that violence is needed to defend our country.

Pair B: You believe that we don't have to use violence to defend our country.

The Judge: You will listen to their reasons.

First, Pair A and Pair B work with your partners. Make a list of your reasons.

Then, exchange ideas with the other pair.

The Judge: Which pair made the better argument?

Culture Corner

Can War Make Peace?

Nonviolence is the law of our species as violence is the law of the brute.

The spirit lies dormant in the brute, and he knows no law but that of physical might.

The dignity of man requires obedience to a higher law—to the strength of the spirit.

Mohandas Gandhi, *Young India* August 11, 1920

Source: san.beck.org/GPJ20-Gandhi.html

Sharing My Ideas *Conflict!*

How can we avoid and resolve conflict in our lives?

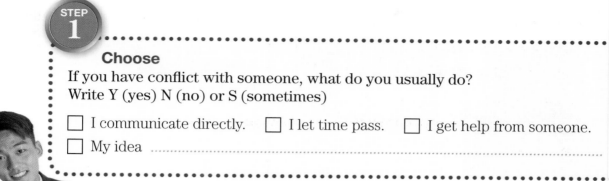

STEP 1

Choose

If you have conflict with someone, what do you usually do?
Write Y (yes) N (no) or S (sometimes)

☐ I communicate directly.   ☐ I let time pass.   ☐ I get help from someone.
☐ My idea ....

STEP 2

Prepare

Tell a story about an experience you have had involving conflict.
Make an outline. Use these questions as a guide.

Speaking notes:

Introduction: (What was the conflict about? With whom? When was the conflict?)

| |
| |

Body: (How did you feel? What did you do? What happened in the end?)

| |
| |

Conclusion: (Did you learn something from this experience? Explain.)

| |
| |

Language Hints:

I once had a fight/argument/disagreement with...

We were fighting/arguing/disagreeing about...

I was very upset/angry.

I felt very helpless/betrayed.

In the end,...

An important lesson I learned was...

STEP 3

Rehearse

Tell your story to a partner.
Give as many details as possible.

 Listener task: Ask for more details: "Please tell me more about... "

STEP 4

Present

Tell your story to a new classmate or to a group.

 Listener task: At the end, tell the speaker how you would feel in this situation.

Presentation Tip:
Speak slowly and calmly.

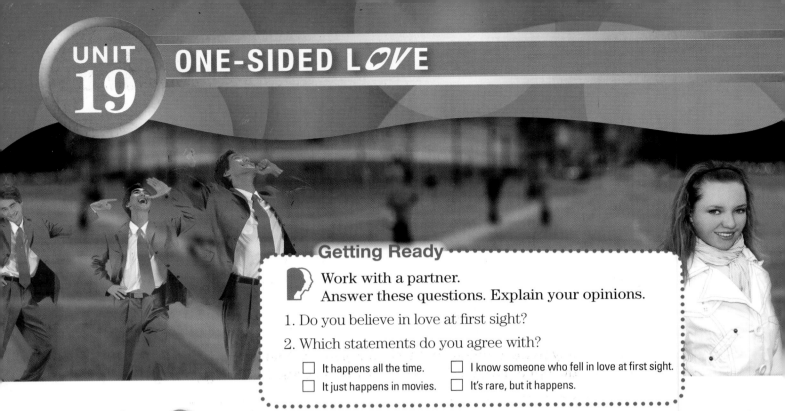

Getting Ready

Work with a partner.
Answer these questions. Explain your opinions.

1. Do you believe in love at first sight?

2. Which statements do you agree with?

☐ It happens all the time.   ☐ I know someone who fell in love at first sight.

☐ It just happens in movies.   ☐ It's rare, but it happens.

Situation 🔊 Track 37

Kevin has fallen in love with someone he doesn't know. But he may be going too far! Listen to Kevin's best friend as he explains the situation.

I am worried about my best friend, Kevin. He's fallen head over heels in love with a woman he doesn't even know. She moved into his apartment building and he says that he fell in love at first sight. He fantasizes about meeting her, going out, getting married, having kids... everything.

I think he's going too far. He started to watch her apartment to learn more about her. He took pictures of her from a distance. He found out her name by looking at her mailbox. (It's Marie Luvlett.) He researched her on the Internet, found her personal Web page and her email address. He says that he's going to ask her out on a date, but that he needs to know more about her first. He thinks that if he finds out more about her, he'll know what to say to impress her.

But I think Kevin is going too far. And honestly, I think he has no chance with her. She's really attractive and I'd be surprised if she doesn't have a boyfriend already. Kevin's a nice guy, but he's shy and has never had a steady girlfriend.

What worries me is that Kevin said he's going to send Marie an email and just sign it "your secret admirer." I think that's kind of cyber-stalking. I think that if he wants to talk to her, he should wait until he sees her and say, "Hi." I think he avoids that because he's too afraid of rejection. But he's convinced that someday she'll fall in love with him.

I don't know what to do. I tried to talk to him about it, but he gets mad. How can I explain to him that this is a totally one-sided love? I'm afraid he's going to go too far and get his feelings hurt, or worse. What he's doing is kind of scary, and if she finds out, she could even call the police. Kevin's harmless, but Marie—and the police—might not see it that way.

Glossary   secret admirer = a person who loves someone from a distance and doesn't reveal his/her identity
cyber-stalking = obsessively bothering or watching someone online   **harmless** = safe; not likely to hurt you

•• Check Your Understanding ••••••••••••••••••••••

Are the sentences true or false? Circle T, F, or NI (not enough information).

1. Kevin fell in love with his neighbor without even talking to her.   T / F / NI
2. Kevin knows almost nothing about the woman he is in love with.   T / F / NI
3. Kevin's friend thinks that Marie probably won't want to go out with Kevin.   T / F / NI
4. Kevin will never ask her out on a date.   T / F / NI
5. Kevin's friend thinks that Kevin may get in trouble with the police.   T / F / NI

What Do You Think? Track 38

A Listen carefully to the opinions of these four people. Who do you agree with most? Rate the opinions from 1 to 4 (1 = strongly agree, 4 = strongly disagree).

☐ **Luis:** Kevin is turning into a stalker. His friend has to do something.

☐ **Ken:** Kevin may be unrealistic, but he hasn't really done anything wrong.

☐ **Yeon-Suk:** Sooner or later, Kevin will forget the woman. His friend shouldn't worry.

☐ **Susan:** His friend should try to introduce him to another woman.

B Work with a classmate.
Talk about the opinions above.

opinionNETWORK

I	agree most	with	Yeon-Suk.
	agree 100 percent		
	kind of agree		Luis.
	sort of agree		
	agree least		Susan.
	completely disagree		

I agree 100 percent with Luis. What about you?

I kind of agree with Ken. Kevin hasn't done anything wrong.

Extending the Topic *Is it love or stalking?*

- Is it possible to love someone too much?
- What is stalking?
- What is a secret admirer?
- How are they different?

A Kevin says it's all for love, but are these things OK? Or are they stalking?

Is it OK for Kevin to...	That's OK.	It depends.	That may be stalking!
look for Marie's name on her mailbox?	☐	☐	☐
send Marie flowers without signing his name?	☐	☐	☐
ask for a date without being introduced first?	☐	☐	☐
search for information about her on the Internet?	☐	☐	☐
take photos of her without her knowing?	☐	☐	☐
follow her?	☐	☐	☐

B Compare your answers with two or three classmates.

BASIC

A: Is it OK for Kevin to look for Marie's name on her mailbox?

B: I think that may be stalking.

EXTENSION

A: Really? I don't think that's so bad.

B: Well, he really shouldn't go near her house if he doesn't know her.

A: I guess if she saw him, she'd think it was strange.

Report your group's ideas to the class. Is Kevin stalking Marie?

Extra Activity *Role play*

Situation: Asking for a first date.

> Person A: You are shy and worried about asking someone to go on a date.
> Person B: You want to help your friend ask for a date.

Person A, ask your friend questions about asking for a date.
For example:
- Should I call, send an email, or ask in person?
- What should I say?
- What if he/she says no?

Practice your role play. Then do your role play conversation in front of another pair.

Culture Corner

How to Deal with a Stalker

Step 1: Seek help. This is a very serious matter.

Step 2: Remove yourself from the stalker's reach.

Step 3: Get a new phone number and make sure it's unlisted.

Step 4: Block your address at the department of motor vehicles and voter registration office.

Step 5: Have your mail delivered to a private post office box.

Step 6: Consider getting a dog if you don't already have one.

Step 7: Get a cellular phone and keep it with you at all times, even inside your home.

Step 8: Document everything.

Step 9: Make several left- or right-hand turns in succession if you think you're being followed while in your car.

Step 10: Consult the local police if you receive a threat. Do not hesitate.

Source: ehow.com

Sharing my Ideas *Make your own love story!*

Give a presentation that tells the story of the perfect romantic meeting. Who meets whom?
Who falls in love? Where? How?

STEP 1

Choose

Select a title for your story:

☐ An Unexpected Meeting   ☐ Love at First Sight   ☐ My idea ....

STEP 2

Prepare

Make an outline of your story:

Speaking notes:

Introduction: (Who is the story about?)

Body: (What happens?   Where does this happen?   How do they feel?)

Conclusion: (How does the story end?)

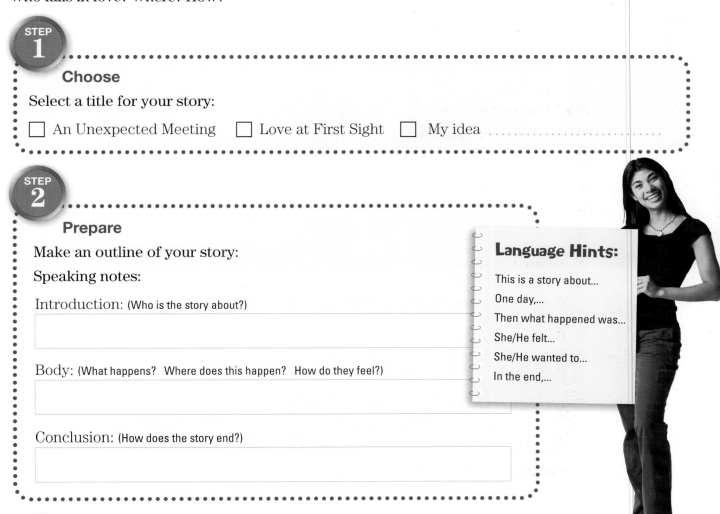

Language Hints:

This is a story about...

One day,...

Then what happened was...

She/He felt...

She/He wanted to...

In the end,...

STEP 3

Rehearse

Work with a partner.
Practice telling your story without
looking at your notes.

 Listener task: After listening
to the story, help your partner
improve the story. (How was
the beginning? Middle? Ending?
Is there enough information?)

STEP 4

Present

Tell your story to a different classmate
or to a group.

 Listener task: After the story,
give feedback: "One thing I
liked about the story is... "

Presentation Tip:
Pause after each sentence. This will help you
keep a good pace.

Getting Ready

Work with a partner.
Answer these questions.

1. Is divorce common in your country?
2. Do you have any friends whose parents are divorced?

Situation Track 39

Kenny is a high-school student. He has just written about his family on his personal website. Listen to his new website entry.

Let me start off by telling everyone that I love my father and mother. They are both really great. But (there are always buts in life, I have learned) there's a BIG problem: they don't love each other anymore. In fact, they hate each other! So they got a divorce last year.

This has really changed my life. Instead of living with my family—my mom and my dad—I live with my dad for one month and then with my mom for a month, and back and forth. First one, then the other one. It's very confusing. Totally upsetting. My high school is close to my dad's house, but my mom's house is pretty far away. She drives me to school, but we have to leave really early, like 5:30 in the morning! So I'm tired all day long. And now I'm not doing well in school. I don't feel like studying. My grades have gone down, but they don't know about that yet. I really don't want to tell them, because it will just cause another big fight.

Anyway, I don't have a home anymore. It's not like I'm homeless or anything, but I'm confused. I just want to be in one place. I want to be part of a real family, not a split family. I wish they would get back together. I really don't understand my parents and I don't think they realize how hard it is for me. They just care about how much time they get to spend with me.

But (didn't I say there are always buts?) there's more. Now my dad has a girlfriend. Well, like he doesn't say she's his girlfriend. He calls her his "special" friend. She spends the night with him sometimes. I think she wants to move in. She's OK, I guess. She's really nice to me. And she's a good cook. My mom keeps asking me about her. She's a little resentful, I think.

Like I said, I'm confused.

Glossary   **divorce** = a legal end of a marriage   **back and forth** = going between two places repeatedly
move in = to start living in a new place   **resentful** = jealous

Check Your Understanding

Answer the questions.

1. Why did Kenny's parents get a divorce?
2. Where does Kenny live now?
3. How has the divorce affected Kenny?
4. What does Kenny want to happen?
5. How does Kenny feel about his dad's "special" friend?

What Do You Think? Track 40

 A Listen carefully to the opinions of these four people.
Check the opinions that you agree with.

☐ **Iris:** Divorce is wrong. Husbands and wives should try hard to stay together.

☐ **Mark:** With or without children, it doesn't matter. When love ends, the marriage is over.

☐ **Anna:** It's OK to get divorced if you don't have children. But if you do have kids, you should never get divorced.

☐ **Shingo:** Divorce may help the children because they don't want to see their parents unhappy or fighting all the time.

 B Work with a classmate.
Discuss your ideas.

opinion NETWORK

Mark	says	that when love ends, the marriage is over.
	thinks	
Do you think	he's right?	
	that's true?	
I	am not sure.	Every situation is different.
	don't know	

Mark thinks that when love ends, the marriage is over. Do you think that's true?

I don't know. Marriage is complicated. Every situation is different.

Extending the Topic *Responding to Kenny*

A Here are some responses to Kenny's entry. Which ones are good responses? How would you respond?

Alladin: Hi, Kenny, I understand your hard life. But even if your parents are divorced, they love you and want you to be happy. Tell them what can make you happy.

Ping: Cheer up, Kenny. Stop worrying about your parents. Live with your dad and be close to your school. Enjoy school life and spend more time with your friends.

Bobo: Well, Kenny, here's my advice. Why don't you live with your mom and sometimes see your dad? Your mom needs you more than your dad does.

One Day: Try to get your parents into counseling. That's the only way they will see the cause of their divorce.

Seed Man: The sooner you forget about your parents, the better. We've got to escape from our parents and their problems.

Justice for All: Hi, Kenny. I think it's important to think about your future, rather than the problems you have now. Study hard and go to college. Figure out what you really want to do.

My response: . . . .

B Work with two or three classmates. Discuss your responses.

BASIC

A: What do you think Kenny should do?

B: I like Ping's advice. He should start focusing on his own life.

EXTENSION

A: But his parents are a big part of his life. He can't just forget about them.

B: No, but if he spends more time on school and with friends, he might not worry so much.

A: Well, I think he should talk to his parents. It's a family problem.

Report your group's ideas to the class. What's the best advice for Kenny?

Culture Corner

Extra Activity *Role play*

Situation: Kenny is tired of living in two places. He is thinking about moving in with his father full-time. He asks his friend for advice.

A: You are Kenny. Tell your friend what you want to do.

B: You are Kenny's friend. Listen to Kenny's situation. Ask questions. Give your advice.

After practicing your role play, do it again in front of other students.

International Comparison of Divorce Rates

Country	Year	Divorce Rate per 1,000 people
Italy	2000	0.6
Greece	2000	0.9
Portugal	2000	1.9
France	1999	2.0
Netherlands	2001	2.1
Japan	2001	2.3
Germany	1999	2.3
Sweden	2000	2.4
Denmark	1999	2.5
U.K.	2000	2.6
Belgium	2000	2.6
Switzerland	2000	2.8
United States	2000	4.1

Source: European Commission and Ministry of Health, Labour and Welfare (Japan)

Sharing My Ideas *Decreasing the divorce rate*

STEP 1

Choose

In many countries, the divorce rate is increasing. Here are some ideas to help slow down the rising divorce rate. Select one idea:

- [ ] Divorce is not allowed, except in certain situations, such as terrible mental illness.
- [ ] The government gives money as a reward to couples who have been married for a long time.
- [ ] The government charges a high tax on divorces.
- [ ] The government hires marriage counselors to give advice to married couples.
- [ ] Couples live together for a few years before they decide to get married.
- [ ] Couples live together, but don't get married.

My idea: ....

STEP 2

Prepare

Make an outline explaining your idea to decrease the divorce rate. Try to convince your audience that your idea is best.

Speaking notes:

Introduction: (What is your idea?)

Body: (Give a list of reasons and examples to support your idea. How will your idea actually stop the increase in divorces?)

Conclusion: (Why is your idea the best solution?)

Language Hints:

Let me explain my plan...

Here is how my plan will work...

This will help...

I believe that...

My guess is that...

This is the best solution because...

Presentation Tip:
Use your voice and body language to help persuade your audience.

STEP 3

Rehearse

Practice with a classmate who has the same idea.

 Listener task:
Do have the same reasons? Do you agree with what your classmate says? How could your classmate's presentation be better?

STEP 4

Present

Present your ideas to a new partner or to a group.

 Listener task: Write one question you would like to ask about your classmate's plan.

Appendix
Personal Opinions

Read each person's opinion about the topic. Fill in the missing words. Note: These are only summaries of the speakers' opinions. To watch the video clips and read the full scripts, go to www.impactseries.com/issues.

Unit 1 – Cosmetic Surgery
Sara

against   happy   popular   rejecting   confident

Cosmetic surgery? Yes, I'm in favor of it. I do understand that the girl's parents are _____ cosmetic surgery. Maybe it feels to them like the girl is rejecting their DNA, or something, that she's actually _____ her parents. And changing the way you look, changing the way that you were naturally born, I mean, that might be heartbreaking for them.

In my country there are a lot of young women who have had cosmetic surgery and it was a really easy process for them. They just went to the clinic and one hour later they came out with big eyes. They felt really beautiful and were really happy. Afterward, they just looked so _____. So cosmetic surgery became really, really _____. First it was the eyes, then the nose, and then other parts of the body. Overall, I think plastic surgery makes many people _____. So I'm for it.

Unit 2 – Friends or Lovers?
Justin

upset   treating   right   friends   sex   ashamed

This is an important topic in terms of modern relationships. In my view, men have to stop treating women as objects. They need to stop _____ women as pretty girls, as decoration. In this case, I think Keiko is right to be shocked and _____. And I think Akira should be _____ of himself. He should write a letter of apology to Keiko.

Maybe he should even invite all their mutual friends together and publicly stand up and say, "I'm sorry, Keiko, for treating you as a _____ object." Good idea, don't you think? Personally, I'd like Keiko and all of her friends and indeed all young women to stand up for their _____ to self-respect, and indeed their right to be _____ and not only lovers with men.

Unit 3 – I Don't Care
Todd

convenient   Earth   environment   weather   love

To me, it's a personal issue. I think that each person needs to consider the effects of global warming, the effects on their _____. Personally, I hate air conditioning. And I guess the fact that my dislike of air conditioning actually helps to fight against global warming is quite _____.

When I'm in Hawaii, I sometimes see people traveling all that way to get to the warm _____, and when they're there, they rent a big car, they roll up their windows and turn on the air conditioning. Now, it just doesn't seem that they _____ nature. I really think that we should all just get back to nature. If we would all get back to nature, we can be healthier and the _____ can be healthier.

Unit 4 – Rules, Rules, Rules
Sun-Hi

rules   rebellious   space   freedom   questionable

In this case, I think the mother deserves more respect. I think that the daughter should listen to her mother more, because she does live in her mother's house, and it seems she has been doing some _____ things, such as smoking, getting bad grades in school, and spending too much money. At the same time, though, I also think the mother should give her some _____ to gain responsibility. Perhaps if she gave her daughter more space, she might follow the _____ more.

In my case, I grew up in a house without too many rules. And I think that experience gave me the space and _____ to be able to be responsible for the things I did. And I think that if I had had more rules growing up, I would have become more _____.

Unit 5 – Plagiarism
Derek

create   product   stealing   thing   different

First of all, we have to understand that plagiarism is cheating. So this situation is a no-brainer. The guy should not be plagiarizing. It's _____, basically. You're stealing someone's ideas.

I guess you can think of plagiarism as stealing a _____, the product being someone's work, someone's effort, put in to _____ a document or some form of information. Plagiarism is the stealing of that product. So in that sense it's really no _____ from stealing someone's product off the shelves, something like bread or fruit or a magazine. You're stealing someone else's product. It's the same _____ if you're stealing music or movies off the Internet or buying pirated software.

Unit 6 – Housework
Justin

wait   marriage   judgment   insist   reasons   refused

Probably the easiest response is that she should just refuse to get married. She should _____ that he help with the housework, and if he doesn't, then they will _____ to get married. But this approach is a bit too easy, I think. In my own case, my father _____ to help with the housework—or he didn't really refuse. He just didn't know how. He sat in his armchair and drank tea, while my mother did the housework. To tell the truth, he didn't even know how to make tea or coffee or vacuum. However, he and my mother had a very happy _____. Their marriage worked. He was charming and funny and a good husband. So perhaps the woman in this case shouldn't make a _____ too quickly.

However, I think it's true that times are changing, and the traditional roles have changed for the better. And I think in this case the woman should ask the man directly why he's refusing to help with the housework. And perhaps if she doesn't like his _____, she could refuse to do other things, like cook for him.

Unit 7 – The Unborn Child
Andrea

responsible   opinions   no   should   have

Since I'm around the same age as the character in the story, I understand that she's confused. She doesn't know what she _____ do. And of course I think that talking to her parents and talking to her boyfriend may help her decide. But it's not necessarily their _____ that she needs to focus on, it's her own.

Is she going to be able to support a child? Is she going to be able to provide it with a loving home? Is she going to be able to be a _____ parent? If the answer is "yes" to all these things, then by all means, _____ the baby. But if even one of them is "_____," is it responsible to have the child and force a person to deal with a complicated life like that? I don't think it is.

Unit 8 – Earning Money
Gillian

positive   quit   choice   old   point

To begin with, for financial reasons, I totally support the woman in taking on two jobs. As long as she finds being an escort or a hostess to be a _____ experience, and she's getting the financial returns that she hopes to, then I have no problems with her decision.

As soon as she finds it demeaning, I think she should

_____ that kind of work. But as a woman, my main _____ is that she has that _____. I don't agree with underage women being involved, and choosing that kind of work, but as an adult I have no problem with it. You're _____ enough to make your own choice.

Unit 9 – Body Art
Mike

unless   pleasure   get   extension   advice

Well, in my opinion, this guy's got a major problem. His girlfriend seems to be a hottie, and he's worried about something as simple as a couple of piercings? What's he thinking? Get over it, _____ you want to lose her.

Body art has been around for thousands of years. It's an _____ of one's self. For most people, it's a private thing, for personal _____ only. Most people never see it. So my _____ to this guy is: go out and _____ a couple of piercings or get a tattoo yourself. But just make sure they're the right ones for you.

Unit 10 – Adult Children
Stacy-Ann

own   selfish   raised   responsibility   take   yourself

What I think is, there is a major misconception about this topic. A lot of young people think that living at home, with your parents, helps you save money and is easier on your lifestyle. But that's a bit too _____. Maybe if you considered how your parents felt about you living at home, it would be different. They wind up having to take care of you more.

And on top of that, your parents have _____ you to get up and get out there on your own, to be on your own. They didn't raise you to live with them forever. Once you're out on your own, you gain a lot of _____ — financially, and emotionally and physically. You learn how to help _____. Realistically, there may come a day when your parents will get up and leave. Decide to retire one day. They're not going to pack you up and _____ you along with them. You're an adult. You have to live on your _____.

Unit 11 – Naomi's Dilemma
Mizuki

professional   feel   different   rejecting   break   comfortable

I agree with her brother. I don't really think it's such a big deal. Of course, I do understand that she doesn't feel very _____ in this situation. She wants to separate her personal life from her _____ life. And, practically speaking, if they date and then they _____ up, things at work could get very difficult.

One problem is that she doesn't know him very well. At the office, he might be nice and polite, but dating is a whole _____ thing. She's not sure if she'll like him in that way. So what I would do is go out for coffee with him and talk about things and then see how they _____ about each other. That way, she's not completely _____ him, and he won't feel that bad. And she might even like him more than she thought she would. Who knows?

Unit 12 – No Place Like Home?
Sara

wall   language   culture   advice   foreigners

I would say this guy is under a lot of stress. It can be stressful for _____ to live in another country, and especially in Japan, in my opinion. I see a lot of foreigners in pubs and night spots in Tokyo, and I guess hanging out there is a kind of relaxation for them, a way for them to get rid of stress.

I have to say, I believe there is like an invisible _____ between the natives here and the foreigners. In my life so far, I've lived once in a country where I spoke the local _____ and once in a country where I didn't speak the local language. I can tell you that I was happier when I was able to speak the language. I was able to experience so many more things, make friends, and appreciate the _____. So my _____ to this guy is that you should study the local language, so you can appreciate the country's culture.

Unit 13 – Career Choice
Mei

stressful   pays   recommend   accomplished   sacrifice

This man has a big decision to make. If I were him, I would definitely work for the big company, the company that _____ a lot. Personally, I used to work for a big company. I did it for eight years and it was a hard job. I had to work a lot of overtime. And sometimes I had to _____ my personal time. For example, I couldn't go out and have dinner with my friends. I couldn't meet my boyfriend.

Things like that made the job very _____, in a way.

And I actually didn't have enough time to sleep, like I was sleeping only four or five hours a night. But when I was done with one of the big projects, I felt really satisfied. I felt like I _____ something really big. And that feeling sort of compensates for everything else. So I would really _____ working for a big company. Overall, it's a good thing.

Unit 14 – Save Our Country
Scott

color   language   citizens   intelligence   nation

It's sort of an immigration issue. Basically, I'm pro-immigration. I think that immigration does help countries develop, in terms of labor, in terms of diversity. Come on, I'm an American. We are a _____ of immigrants, so of course I'm very pro-immigration.

However, immigration does create some tensions. Like, I'm from a part of the country where there are many Latinos, some of whom come into the country illegally. Sometimes I think, well, if you want to be here, you need to do like my ancestors did. Come in legally, learn the _____, learn more about the country, and then if you want to become _____ and you want the same rights as we have, then that's fine. I guess that's how I feel. It has nothing to do with _____ or whether they should be there based on skin _____. Those arguments are really silly to me.

Unit 15 – High-tech Toys
Todd

realize   important   date   less   human

I guess I sympathize with both of them. I mean, wouldn't it be great if all couples had the same interests? But it's not possible. And it may not even be what's most important in a relationship. But what is _____ from this story is that the man has to _____ that the woman is not interested in his computer talk. In his high-tech-toys talk.

So he needs to do what she suggests: close the computer and have a conversation and try to reconnect with her. Try to reconnect with what brought them together in the first place. Go out on a _____ with her. It's not the same thing to download a movie as it is to go out and experience society outside together. Go to a movie and then after that go to dinner. Be with other people. That's a way to bring back a _____ aspect to all of this. I mean, technology helps us to do a whole lot. Technology is great for many, many things. But it also makes us a little _____ human sometimes.

Unit 16 – A Woman's Place

Derek

equal   career   ability   stigma   power

This is an equality issue. Basically, the foundation of modern society needs to be based upon the idea that a man and a woman are _____. And both have the _____ to go and do and see and have what they want. Obviously, this doesn't mean infringing upon the feelings and rights of others, but a woman should have the ability to choose and do as she wants.

If a woman prefers to stay at home and be with her family—to stay at home and raise her children, there should be no _____ attached to that. The same as if a woman wants to work, and raise a family at the same time, more _____ to her. And especially if a woman just wants to choose a _____ over family, that's her choice.

Unit 17 – The Art of Compromise

Gillian

learn   divorce   relationship   gender   one

It's clear that these two have a major problem. I mean, Cheryl thinks Sam should fix things around the house, and he doesn't and he says he can't. And Sam thinks Cheryl should cook, and she doesn't, and she says she can't. Well, one thing they could do is get a _____. End it.

But I think there's another way. I'm all for them sitting down, talking about what they like to do in their _____. And then if they need training or re-education, go to a cooking class or get a do-it-yourself handbook. They can learn their role. Or learn different roles. They need to _____ to do different things in their family. Maybe there isn't _____ set role for a man, one set role for a woman. And maybe they're finding this out because they can't do anything at the moment. They're sort of paralyzed. So I think it's time for them to try other _____ roles.

Unit 18 – Can War Make Peace?

Mike

army   know   survive   peaceful   views   struggle

I know a little bit about the topic of war and peace. I'm from Ireland. And we've had 600 years of struggle and difficulty. Ireland was an occupied country for most of our history, whether it was by the Vikings or Normans or British. But it makes you think about some questions: what is war and peace? How do we _____ real peace? You can be an occupied country and be "at peace." But are you really at peace?

I sympathize with this child. I realize he's in a very difficult position. He has different _____ from his family and he lives a very difficult life. What's he going to do?

You know, he'll probably grow up and end up joining the _____. And maybe for moral reasons, he'll probably try to do as little as possible in the way of violence. That's the way he'll _____. Life's a _____, but this boy's struggle is harder than most of ours. In my opinion, we need not to fight as much as we do. We need to be more _____.

Unit – 19 One-sided Love

Kyle

weird   know   about   move   followed

Personally, I know what it's like to be attracted to girls. I am attracted to them, and I try to meet as many girls as possible. But I do it where I talk to them and try to get to _____ them first. And I want them to get to know me, to see if we're compatible because I believe that getting to know the girl is what it's all _____—not trying to get to know them before you've even spoken to them.

Men or women, no one wants to be _____ and not spoken to because that can come off as creepy. Or you might think you're being stalked and that can get you in trouble. This guy might have a problem with that. He might come off like he's stalking her and she might feel _____ and get the cops. If I were his friend, I would definitely talk to him. I'd be like, dude, if you want to talk to her, then talk to her. If you're not going to do anything about it, you should just _____ on, and not scare her away, because that's not going to get you anywhere.

Unit 20 – My Split Family

Scott

thinking   hard   love   moved   careful

This is somewhat personal for me. I feel that as a child of a family that's gone through—and not just one divorce but many divorces—I think it's very _____ on the children when a divorce happens. I'm not saying that a couple shouldn't divorce. What I am saying is that if you have children, you really need to be _____ about the effect that has on the children.

In my case too, I was _____ around every weekend. You know, I would see my father and then I would go back for part of the week to my mother—back and forth, back and forth! And it was really hard. I assume they were trying their best but, in some ways, they were just _____ about themselves and not how it made us kids feel. So, I'm not saying don't divorce. In fact, I'm happy that my parents are divorced because they didn't get along and they didn't _____ each other at that point, but it didn't affect me in a good way.

Vocabulary

Study these vocabulary words before or after you work on each unit.

 Definitions come from *Longman Dictionary of Contemporary English*.

Unit 1

approach – to move towards or nearer to someone or something

attract – to make someone interested in something

beg – to ask for something in an anxious or urgent way, because you want it very much

big deal – an important or exciting event or situation

cosmetic surgery – medical operations that improve your appearance after you have been injured, or because you want to look more attractive

drastic – extreme and sudden

eyelids – a piece of skin that covers your eye when it is closed

fix – to repair something that is broken or not working properly

old-fashioned – someone who is old-fashioned has ideas or attitudes that were more usual in the past than now

self-esteem – the feeling of being satisfied with your own abilities and that you deserve to be liked or respected

wit – the ability to say things that are clever and amusing

Unit 2

confused – unable to think clearly about what someone is saying or what is happening

couple – two people who are married or having a sexual or romantic relationship

kiss goodnight – kissing someone to say goodbye at the end of the evening or before going to bed

lovers – people who are involved romantically with each other

natural – normal and as you would expect

romantic – relating to feelings of love or a loving relationship

spend time – to use time doing a particular thing or pass time in a particular place

Unit 3

air conditioner – a machine that makes the air in a room or building cooler and drier

carbon dioxide – the gas produced when animals breathe out, when carbon is burned in air, or when animal or vegetable substances decay

chill(ed) – if you chill something such as food or drink, or if it chills, it becomes very cold but does not freeze

chill out – to relax completely instead of feeling angry, tired or nervous

get (it) – to understand something

global warming – a general increase in world temperatures caused by increased amounts of carbon dioxide around the Earth

scientist – someone who works or is trained in science

setting – the position in which you put the controls on a machine or instrument

temperature – a measure of how hot or cold a place or thing is

the planet – the world, used especially when talking about the environment

Who cares? – used to say that something does not worry or upset you because it is not important

Unit 4

acceptable – acceptable behavior is considered to be morally or socially good enough

fed up with – annoyed or bored, and wanting something to change

grade – a mark that a student is given for their work or for an examination

ignore – to deliberately pay no attention to something that you have been told or that you know about

impossible (person) – behaving in a very unreasonable and annoying way

push someone – to encourage or force someone to do something or to work hard

strict – expecting people to obey rules or to do what you say

terrible – extremely bad

Unit 5

copy – to deliberately make or produce something that is exactly like another thing

fail – to not pass a test or examination

get in trouble – do something that causes you to be scolded or punished

give the impression – create the belief that something is true

injury – a wound or damage to part of your body caused by an accident or attack

inspiration – a person, experience or source that gives you new ideas for something you do

kick someone out – to make someone leave a place, job, etc.

plagiarize – when someone uses another person's words, ideas, or work and pretends they are their own

reference – part of something you say or write in which you mention a person or thing

report – to tell the police or someone in authority that an accident or crime has happened

word for word – in exactly the same words

Unit 6

calculate – to find out how much something will cost or how long something will take by using numbers

duties – things you have to do as part of your job

finances – the money that an organization or person has, and the way that they manage it

housework – work that you do to take care of a house — for example, washing or cleaning

old-fashioned – not considered to be modern or fashionable any more

persuade – to make someone decide to do something, especially by giving them reasons why they should do it, or asking them many times to do it

postpone – to change the date or time of a planned event or action to a later one

professional – someone who earns money by doing a job, sport or activity

responsible job – an important job, a meaningful job

Unit 7

abortion – a medical operation to end a pregnancy

deny – to say that something is not true, or that you do not believe something

(my) heart is torn – to have divided emotions, to be unclear on what to decide

horrified – to be very shocked and upset or afraid

pregnant – if a woman or female animal is pregnant, she has an unborn baby growing inside her body

rape – to force someone to have sex, especially by using violence

regret – to feel sorry about something you have done and wish you had not done

responsibility – a duty to be in charge of someone or something

shocked – feeling surprised and upset by something very unexpected and unpleasant

solution – a way of solving a problem or dealing with a difficult situation

traditional – following ideas and methods that have existed for a long time, rather than doing anything new or different

Unit 8

confess – to admit something that you feel embarrassed about

day job – a job a person does during normal working hours

escort – someone who is paid to go out with someone socially

future husband – a man I will get married to someday

in good shape – physically fit

the rush – the time in the day, month or year when a place or group of people is particularly busy

Unit 9

be down/look down – be or look unhappy or sad

behind the times – old-fashioned

cheap – showing a lack of honesty, moral principles, or sincere feelings, so that you do not deserve respect

hot – someone who is hot is very attractive sexually

loosen up – to stop worrying and become more relaxed

minor – small and not very important or serious

overreact – to react to something with too much emotion, or by doing something that is unnecessary

piercing – a hole made through part of your body so that you can put jewelry there

pushy – someone who is pushy does everything they can to get what they want from others – used in order to show disapproval

turn someone on – to make someone feel sexually excited

weird – very strange and unusual, and difficult to understand

Unit 10

boomerang – a curved stick that flies in a circle and comes back to you when you throw it; first used in Australia

creepy – making you feel nervous and slightly frightened

materialistic – concerned only with money and possessions, rather than things of the mind such as art, religion, or moral beliefs; used in order to show disapproval

parasite – a lazy person who does not work but depends on other people – used to show disapproval

phenomenon – something that happens or exists in society, science or nature, especially something that is studied because it is difficult to understand

spoiled – a spoiled person, especially a child, is rude and behaves badly because they have always been given what they want and allowed to do what they want

trend – a general tendency in the way a situation is changing or developing

Unit 11

get ahead – to be successful and do better than other people in a job or work

give something a shot – make an attempt to do something or achieve something, especially something difficult

inappropriate – not suitable or right for a particular purpose or in a particular situation

mess something up – to spoil or ruin something, especially something important or something that has been carefully planned

sexual harassment – sexual remarks, looks, or touching done to someone who does not want it, especially from someone they work with

update – to tell someone the most recent information about a situation

Unit 12

culture shock – the feeling of being confused or anxious that you get when you visit a foreign country or a place that is very different from the one you are used to

enthusiasm – a strong feeling of interest and enjoyment about something and an eagerness to be involved in it

"go native" – to behave, dress, or speak like the people who live in the country where you have come to stay or work; often used humorously

hassle – something that is annoying, because it causes problems or is difficult to do

narrow-minded – unwilling to accept or understand new or different ideas, opinions, or customs

open-minded – willing to consider and accept other people's ideas and opinions

patriot – someone who loves their country

take advantage of – to use a particular situation to do or get what you want

Unit 13

benefits – extra money or other advantages that you get as part of your job or from insurance that you have

dump – to get rid of waste material

dynamic – full of energy and new ideas, and determined to succeed

kid – to say something that is not true, especially as a joke

move up – to get a better job in a company, or change to a more advanced group, higher rank, or higher level

naive – not having much experience of how complicated life is, so that you trust people too much and believe that good things will always happen

progressive – supporting new or modern ideas and methods, especially in politics and education

promotion – a move to a more important job or position in a company or organization

scandal – an event in which someone, especially someone important, behaves in a bad way that shocks people

socially responsible – caring about the well-being of society and the environment

status – respect and importance that someone or something is given

Unit 14

citizens – someone who legally belongs to a particular country and has rights and responsibilities there, whether they are living there or not

election – when people vote to choose someone for an official position

enemy – someone who hates you and wants to harm you

glorious – having or deserving great fame, praise, and honor

immigrants – someone who enters another country to live there permanently

prejudice – an unreasonable dislike and distrust of people who are different from you in some way, especially because of their race, sex, religion, etc. – used to show disapproval

race – one of the main groups that humans can be divided into according to the color of their skin and other physical features

rights – things that you are morally, legally, or officially allowed to do or have

vote – to choose somebody or something in an election

Unit 15

convenience – the quality of making something easier or saving you time

download – to move information or programs from a computer network to an individual computer

high-tech – using advanced technology

network – a set of computers that are connected to each other so that they can share information

snuggle – to settle into a warm, comfortable position

stroll – to walk somewhere in a slow, relaxed way

virtual – made, done, or seen on the Internet or on a computer, rather than in the real world

Unit 16

belief – the feeling that something is definitely true or definitely exists

controversial – causing a lot of disagreement, because many people have strong opinions about the subject being discussed

guidance – help and advice that is given to someone about their work, education, or personal life

ideal – the best or most suitable that something could possibly be

out-of-date – if something is out-of-date, it is no longer considered useful or effective, because something more modern exists

raise children – to look after your children and help them grow

role – the way in which someone or something is involved in an activity or situation

society – people in general, considered in relation to the laws and organizations that make it possible for them to live together

spouse – a husband or wife

suited – having the right qualities for a particular purpose

Unit 17

assume – to think that something is true, although you do not have definite proof

compromise – to reach an agreement in which everyone involved accepts less than what they wanted at first

disaster – something that is very bad or a failure, especially when this is very annoying or disappointing

klutz – someone who drops things and falls easily

knitting – to make clothing out of yarn, using knitting needles

retirement – when you stop working, usually because of your age

sewing – the activity or skill of making or repairing clothes or decorating cloth with a needle and thread

Unit 18

ashamed – feeling embarrassed and guilty because of something you have done

bomb – to attack a place by leaving a bomb there, or by dropping bombs on it from a plane

bully – someone who uses their strength or power to frighten or hurt someone who is weaker

childish – behaving in a silly way that makes you seem much younger than you really are; used to show disapproval

destroy – to damage something so badly that it no longer exists or cannot be used or repaired

dignity – the fact of being respected or deserving respect

human right – one of the basic rights that many societies think every person should have to be treated in a fair and equal way

injustice – a situation in which people are treated very unfairly and not given their rights

nightmare – a very difficult, unpleasant, or frightening experience or situation

victim – someone who suffers because of something bad that happens or because of an illness

Unit 19

cyber-stalking – obsessively tracking someone's behavior online

fantasize – to imagine that you are doing something that is very pleasant or exciting, but which is very unlikely to happen

harmless – unable or unlikely to hurt anyone or cause damage

head over heels (in love) – to love or suddenly start to love someone very much

one-sided – an activity or competition that is one-sided is one in which one person or side is much stronger or does much more than the other

rejection – a situation in which someone stops giving you love or attention

secret admirer – someone who likes a person and thinks that they are attractive, but doesn't reveal his or her feelings

stalking – the crime of following and watching someone over a period of time in a way that is annoying or threatening

steady (boy/girlfriend) – someone you have been having a romantic relationship with for a long time

Unit 20

back and forth – going in one direction and then in the opposite direction, and repeating this several times

counseling – advice and support given by a counselor to someone with problems, usually after talking to them

divorce – the legal ending of a marriage

move in – to start living in a new home

resentful – feeling angry and upset about something that you think is unfair

split family – a family that is divided into different groups

upset – to make someone feel unhappy or worried

Welcome to the *Impact* Series
Something for everyone's teaching and learning needs

Dynamic Conversation Series

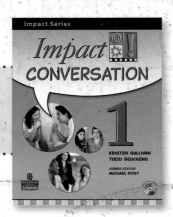
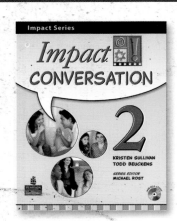

Cutting-Edge Discussion Series

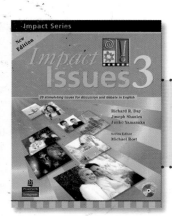

Innovative Listening Series

Coursebook Series

Grammar and Vocabulary Skills

www.impactseries.com